7.50

Please return on or before the last date stamped below

✓5
✓18

Library, Dinnington Campus
Rotherham College
Doe Quarry Lane, Dinnington, S25 2NF
Renewals/Enquiries: 01909 559279

To my mother, Nora Moran, who encouraged us to believe that a good question is better than a standard answer, and to my late nephew, Tristan, RIP, who inspired me in countless ways

Managing Your Own Learning at University

A Practical Guide

AIDAN P. MORAN

University College Dublin Press
Preas Choláiste Ollscoile Bhaile Átha Cliath

First published 1997 by University College Dublin Press,
Newman House, St. Stephen's Green, Dublin 2, Ireland
Revised edition 2000
Reprinted 2006

© Aidan P. Moran 1997, 2000
Illustrations © Shane Sutton 1997
ISBN 1 900621 58 4

Cataloguing in Publication data available from the British Library

Designed by Origin Design Associates, Dublin
Illustrations by Shane Sutton
Index by Helen Litton
Typeset in 10/11.5 Garamond and Gill Sans by
Seton Music Graphics, Bantry, Co. Cork, Ireland
Printed and bound in Great Britain by
Athenaeum Press Ltd., Gateshead, Tyne & Wear

Contents

Preface and Acknowledgements

Going to university is a daunting experience for many students. In particular, they are confronted with a number of educational and personal challenges for which they have had little or no formal training in school. They have to adjust to new methods of teaching such as the lecture technique, to different criteria of academic evaluation, to changes in the amount and type of background reading required for the more independent form of study and, above all, to the fact that they have to take responsibility for 'managing their own learning' in planning, conducting and evaluating their own academic work in university. But these challenges may be viewed as *opportunities* to acquire new skills, such as learning to concentrate while studying, rather than as threats to entrenched habits of learning. Therefore, the purpose of this book is to help students to take a more active role in their own education by learning not only *how* to learn effectively but also how to *think* for themselves. And with the inclusion of a chapter on 'Critical Thinking' (Chapter 7), my book differs from other popular texts on 'study skills'. It is also unique in its explicit attempt to explain the cognitive psychological principles on which effective learning strategies are based.

I have organised the book so that each chapter addresses a different educational challenge or 'learning skill' in university. To begin with, in Chapter 1, I explore the task of 'managing your own learning' which involves becoming an active, independent and self-motivated student. Then, in successive chapters, I address such skills as motivating oneself to study (Chapter 2), organising one's study time properly (Chapter 3), taking lecture notes efficiently (Chapter 4), reading for maximum understanding (Chapter 5), improving concentration skills (Chapter 6), thinking critically about what one hears and reads (Chapter 7), understanding and remembering what one learns (Chapter 8), planning and writing research assignments (Chapter 9), and doing one's best in examinations (Chapter 10).

This book would not have been possible without the help of many colleagues and friends. Therefore, I wish to acknowledge with sincere gratitude the assistance which I received from the following people:

Barbara Mennell (Executive Editor, UCD Press) for her constructive suggestions and consistent encouragement; John Conboy (for his technical assistance) and Gillian Martin (for research assistance).

I also wish to thank the following colleagues from University College Dublin, who responded promptly and generously to a research questionnaire which I used to gather information for this book: Dr Joe Brady (Geography), Professor Niamh Brennan (Accountancy), Dr Ann Breslin (Physics), Mr Paul Brown (Teaching Development Unit), Professor Mary Burke (Library and Information Studies), Mr Joe Carthy (Computer Science), Ms Blanaid Clarke (Law), Mr Victor Connerty (Classics), Ms Gerardine Doyle (Accountancy), Dr Declan Gilheaney (Chemistry), Professor Hugh Gough (History), Dr Johnnie Gratton (French), Dr Pat Guiry (Chemistry), Mr. Seamus Heslin (formerly of Economics), Mr George Hilton (Veterinary Medicine), Dr Tom Inglis (Sociology), Dr Miriam Kennedy (Teaching Development Unit), Dr Gerardine Meaney (English), Dr Pauline Mellon (Mathematics), Mr Feargal Murphy (Linguistics), Professor Peter Neary (Economics), Dr Michael O'Connell (Psychology), Dr Mark O'Reilly (Psychology), Mr Robert Pearce (formerly of Library and Information Studies), Dr Patrick Purcell (Civil Engineering), Professor Hugh Ridley (German), Dr Mark Richardson (Civil Engineering), Professor Pat Shannon (Geology), Dr Therese Smith (Music), Dr Barbara Traxler-Brown (Library and Information Studies), Mr Colm Tobin (Careers Office) and Professor Harry White (Music). I am indebted for similar reasons to the following colleagues from Trinity College, Dublin: Dr Johan Dehantschutter (Geology), Dr E. Finch (Physics), Dr Ray Fuller (Psychology) and Dr Shane O'Mara (Psychology).

Next, I wish to thank current and former Deans (especially Professor Philip Bourke, Professor Fergus D'Arcy, Professor Gerard Doyle and Professor Mary Lambkin) in University College Dublin, for inviting me to contribute to their annual 'study skills' seminars for students. Also, I am very grateful to Professor Terry Dolan (Old and Middle English), Ms Aine Galvin (New ERA programme, UCD), Mr Jim Gourley (Tutorial Services, UK), Mr Philip Harvey (Campus Bookshop), Ms Olive Keogh (*The Irish Times*), Dr Sarah Moore (University of Limerick) and Mr John Quinn (Radio Telefís Éireann) for their interest in my work. Finally, I wish to thank my mother, Nora Moran, my brothers (Ciaran and Dermot), my sister (Patricia), my late nephew, Tristan, RIP, and my friends (especially Angela, Brendan, Brendan and Neil) for their love and support at all times.

Aidan P. Moran
Dublin, September 2000

1. Going to University: The Challenge of Managing Your Own Learning

'Education is one of the few things that a person is willing to pay for and not get'
(W. L. Bryan)

Introduction

Going to university is an exciting yet daunting experience for many students. The excitement comes not only from the adventure of exploring interesting subjects in a stimulating educational environment but also from the fun of making new friends and acquiring different skills and interests in a challenging setting. Unfortunately, this expansion of your intellectual and social horizons does not come without a price. In this regard, I'm *not* referring to the financial cost of your books, accommodation and living and travel expenses. Instead, what I have in mind is the daunting *psychological* challenge that you face when studying any subject in university. Specifically, in order to get a successful academic education, you will have to accept *personal responsibility* for a task for which you have received little or no special training in school. This task requires you to *manage your own learning* or to become an active, independent and self-motivated student in planning, conducting and evaluating your academic work. Accepting this challenge means that you will have to become a *driver* rather than a passenger in your journey through university. Therefore, the purpose of this book is to give you some 'driving lessons' in learning. And the first lesson concerns the type of learning that is required of you in university.

This chapter is organised as follows. To begin with, I shall explain the nature and characteristics of active learning. Then, I shall help you to evaluate your current study habits in order to determine whether they reveal an accidental or a deliberate approach to learning. Next, I shall introduce a central theme of this book – the idea that effective study requires reading with a purpose: namely, to obtain specific answers to specific questions. Then, I shall provide a brief overview of the academic challenges which you can expect to face in university. These challenges include such tasks as motivating yourself to get down to study (Chapter 2), organising your study time properly (Chapter 3), taking lecture notes efficiently (Chapter 4), reading for maximum understanding (Chapter 5), learning to concentrate deeply (Chapter 6), thinking critically about your subject (Chapter 7), understanding and remembering what you learn (Chapter 8), planning, researching and writing formal assignments (Chapter 9), and preparing adequately for examinations (Chapter 10). Finally, I shall try to answer an important practical question: What are the distinctive skills of students who are successful academically?

At first glance, many of the academic skills covered in this book may seem familiar to you. After all, you would not be attending university now if you had not shown some prior competence in studying at second-level. But it is a big mistake to assume that the learning habits that you have developed in school will automatically guarantee academic success for you in university. For a start, do you think that you will you be able to motivate yourself to study in the absence of such familiar school 'props' as a limited number of textbooks, a well-structured syllabus and daily inspection of your homework? In addition, are you prepared for the fact that the amount of time that you will spend in lectures is relatively low compared to that which you are expected to spend in private study? Clearly, this situation is quite different from what you experienced in school. Furthermore, how will you know when to give your own opinions of topics or theories rather than a summary of what is contained in your textbooks? Not surprisingly, the success of your education in university will depend on the way in which you answer these questions. And that is why universities are paradoxical – they bring out the *best* and *worst* qualities in students simultaneously. To explain, if you're not prepared to take responsibility for your own learning, university will be a frustrating and unpleasant experience for you. But if you relish the challenge of developing new knowledge and skills, then your time in university will never be boring. The choice is yours. So, are you prepared to take some driving lessons in learning?

Learning: Active and passive

The term 'learning' refers to a relatively permanent change in our knowledge and/or our behaviour as a result of some past experience. For example, consider how we learn to drive a car. In this case, the experience is a programme of driving lessons, the change in knowledge involves an increased understanding of the rules of the road and the change in behaviour refers to the skills of actually starting, steering and stopping the car safely. But it would be a mistake to assume that the understanding and 'doing' parts of behaviour can ever be separated completely. They tend to go hand-in-hand. For example, learning to play tennis requires both conceptual knowledge (understanding the rules of the game so that you can keep the score) and procedural skills (actually hitting the ball over the net).

Although we consciously try to master driving or tennis skills, other types of learning are not so deliberate. For example, learning can occur *accidentally* or implicitly as well as purposefully. To explain, learning is deliberate if it is motivated by a clear and specific purpose (e.g. looking up the name of the Shakespearean character who says 'To be or not to be . . .') whereas it is accidental if it happens by chance (e.g. stumbling across the little known fact that most clocks using Roman numerals mistakenly employ 'iiii' rather than 'iv' to designate '4'). By the way, as a test of your incidental learning ability, do you know the name of the publisher of this book? No? Well, look for it now!

This contrast between deliberate and accidental learning is not just an academic distinction – it has profound practical significance. Specifically, research shows that the knowledge produced by a *deliberate intention* to find out something is richer, better linked with what we already know and more durable than that yielded by random discovery. Thus Kolodner (1997) concluded that 'modern educational theory stemming from research in the cognitive sciences indicates that knowledge gained through activity . . . is more usable than is knowledge gained through memorization' (p. 57). As we shall see, this finding explains why *active questioning* (e.g. 'what exactly am I trying to find out here?') before you read a book promotes deeper understanding of the material than does passive reading of it. Of course, accidental learning (such as 'surfing the net' on your computer) can be valuable also. For example, the history of science is replete with cases of serendipity, where people capitalised on chance events. Thus George de Mestral invented the 'velcro' fastener after he had noticed that burs stuck to his clothing (Cryer, 1996). But significantly, such apparent strokes of luck tend to occur for people who are *already* 'primed' to seek an answer to a pressing problem. Therefore, there is a lot of truth in the old saying that luck happens 'when preparation meets opportunity' or that 'fortune favours the prepared mind' (which is attributed to Louis Pasteur).

Becoming an active learner: Attitude and skills

So far, I've been extolling the merits of active learning. But how can you become a more active learner than you are at present? As we shall see, this task requires two steps. First, you will have to change your attitude to study. Specifically, you will have to take responsibility for your own study behaviour – something which I shall address shortly. And second, you will have to develop a set of learning skills (which will be covered in the remaining chapters of this book). Unfortunately, both of these steps are hampered by our experience of second-level education. For example, in school you probably believed that it was the teacher's job to get you through your course work. And so, he or she told you what to learn. Not surprisingly, you spent most of your time absorbing the *products* of other people's thoughts (e.g. ideas like scientific theories) rather than exploring the *process* by which your own mind works. But things are different in university. For instance, on the basis that you've passed certain exams and have reached adulthood, you are assumed know *how* to learn. But is this assumption valid? To answer this question, my colleagues and I conducted a survey of the academic experiences and problems of 1100 first-year students from different faculties in an Irish university (Moran *et al.*, 1991). We found that almost *one third* of this sample reported that they had encountered significant difficulties in organising, getting down to and concentrating on their studies in their first six months in university. Furthermore, 41 per cent of these First Years expressed considerable anxiety about the amount and quality of their learning. Clearly, these motivational difficulties and learning problems in otherwise bright students suggest that the transition from school to university is not as smooth as had been assumed. And part of this 'transition problem' is caused by a naive attitude to learning. For example, many students make excuses ('We had a bad lecturer' or 'The wrong questions came up for me') when they perform poorly in examinations. But by evading responsibility in this manner, they prevent themselves from working on their weaknesses. Not surprisingly, students who make lots of excuses in their work rarely fulfil their academic potential in university. By contrast, successful students tend to make goals – not excuses. They realise the wisdom of the sporting maxim that 'winners are workers'. And perhaps the best place to start your work is by evaluating your current study habits.

Evaluating your study habits

In order to improve any skill, you have to begin by finding out how well you can perform it at present. Therefore, in Box 1.1, I would like you to establish whether your current study habits reflect a 'deliberate' or an 'accidental' approach to learning. If you answer 'yes' to most of these questions in Box 1.1, then your present study habits are probably quite efficient and there is little need to change the way in which you approach your academic assignments. However, if you

> ### Box 1.1   *Are you an accidental or a deliberate learner?*
>
> Consider your present study habits. In order to find out if they reflect accidental or deliberate learning processes, please answer either 'yes' or 'no' to the following study questions. Answer these questions honestly as there is no point in fooling yourself. Remember – it's *your* learning which is at stake.
>
> ### Question
>
> 1. *Do you have a clear plan or timetable for your studies each day? (y/n)*
>
> 2. *Do you write down specific questions on a blank sheet of paper before you read a book/article which you wish to study? (y/n)*
>
> 3. *Before you read a chapter, do you flick through it to get a quick overview of what it's about? (y/n)*
>
> 4. *Do you check your progress as you study by asking yourself how the new material relates to what you already know? (y/n)*
>
> 5. *Do you always write summaries of important points as you read a book? (y/n)*
>
> 6. *When you have finished studying, do you take a moment to review what you have learned? (y/n)*

answered 'no' to most of these questions, then your current study habits are more likely to be *accidental* than deliberate. This finding suggests that you are not fulfilling your learning potential. Therefore, what you need most is a practical way of making your learning *more deliberate* than it is at present. One way of doing this is to ask questions before you read something which you wish to learn. This act of questioning can transform aimless reading into deliberate studying – a key issue which I shall return to in Chapter 5.

Reading, studying and questioning

Have you ever heard someone saying that they are 'reading' English or some other subject in university? Clearly, such people regard reading and studying as equivalent terms. After all, both activities seem to involve the skill of processing information from books or other written material. But although these terms overlap to some extent, they refer to different processes. To explain, cognitive psychologists (who explore how our minds work in acquiring, storing and using knowledge) have discovered that studying is a more complex mental activity than reading. In particular, it involves deliberate or active learning (i.e. trying to find the answer to some specific question) whereas reading is a more passive and automatic process. To illustrate this difference between reading and studying, imagine what would happen if you approached a textbook as if it were a novel. Opening the first page, you would sit down and begin to read the pages sequentially. And because you are reading it as if it were a novel, you would not take any notes. Unfortunately, unless you are gripped by the drama of textbooks, your mind would begin to wander after a few minutes. Why? Because textbooks were *not designed* to be read like novels – they were meant to be consulted rather than processed at one sitting. Accordingly, textbooks contain features (e.g. a table of contents, a reference section and a subject index) which are not found in novels. These features enable textbooks to be *interrogated* by people who are looking for specific answers to specific questions (e.g. What caused the famine in Ireland in the 1840s?).

Studying is reading with a purpose – to obtain specific answers to specific questions

Research shows that the best way to approach a textbook is to look upon it as something which you *consult* when you are *looking for something*. That something is the answer to a question which you have posed. For example, in biology, what is photosynthesis? How does it work? In order to answer these questions, you look for a biology textbook, flick through it until you obtain relevant information and only then, proceed to make appropriate summary notes. Leaving that textbook aside, you are now ready to repeat the same steps with a different biology book. Comparing the answers you obtained to the same question (namely what is photosynthesis?) is the first step in learning. Using this example, we can see that studying always involves *questioning* whereas reading for leisure is a more passive activity. And as the famous educationalist, John Dewey, once observed: 'Passivity is the opposite of thought'.

So, the habit of questioning before reading is what separates successful students from less successful peers. Indeed, it could be argued that successful students are people with questions in search of answers, whereas lazy or uninterested students are people who have pre-packaged answers in search of questions. I shall return to this idea in Chapter 5 when exploring the PQRR reading technique (see p. 60). But apart from not specifying questions before they read, unsuccessful students also display other bad habits when faced with the task of learning from textbooks. For example, they tend to read the material straight through without slowing down when they reach difficult sections. By contrast, successful students tend to monitor their understanding, re-read difficult sections of the material and pause from time to time in order to review what they have learned (Whimbey, 1976). Some of the faulty learning habits of unsuccessful students are summarised in Box 1.2.

As I explained above, the main purpose of studying is to obtain specific answers to specific questions. By analogy, acting involves more than just rattling off a playwright's words as fast as possible. It involves conveying the *character* suggested by the script as much as the meaning of the words themselves. Likewise, studying is a deeper process than reading. In particular, effective studying is a form of learning which is motivated by the attempt to obtain *specific* answers to *specific* questions. The practical implication of this idea is that unless we have specific questions guiding our studies, we are likely to waste a lot of valuable time when we pore over our books. Overall, therefore, psychology shows us that effective studying depends on our ability to identify or formulate appropriate *questions* for ourselves. Without questions, our reading is likely to be random and aimless – rather like a car driving around in circles.

| Box 1.2 | *What can your reading habits tell us about your likely academic success?* |

Reading a Textbook

Successful students *Active approach*	Unsuccessful students *Passive approach*
1. Use questions to guide their reading (e.g. turn chapter and paragraph headings into questions for themselves)	*Read without any questions*
2. Flick back and forth between the pages	*Read the material in strict chronological sequence*
3. Slow down when they encounter difficulty. Re-read difficult sections	*Go at same pace regardless of difficulty of material*
4. Check their understanding/ monitor progress regularly	*Rarely check understanding or monitor progress*

The importance of asking questions

So far, I have suggested that studying is a questioning activity. But why is questioning so important for effective learning?

According to psychologists, questioning facilitates learning for a number of reasons. Firstly, setting questions helps to narrow the focus of your mind so that you can concentrate more effectively as you read. In fact, the more specific the question, the narrower will be your attentional focus and the richer your memory. Indeed, Deese & Deese (1994) go so far as to say that 'most things worth remembering are answers to some sort of questions' (p. 45). Secondly, memory research shows that active questioning (e.g. what is the main point being made here?) leads to a *richer memory and understanding* of information than does passive transcription of it. This 'depth of processing' phenomenon is particularly noticeable for questions which have a strong relevance to oneself. To illustrate, consider the *self-reference effect* in cognitive psychology. This term refers to the finding that people remember more information when they try to relate it to themselves than when they simply try to learn it off by heart as 'neutral' knowledge. You can explore this effect for yourself by performing the exercise in Box 1.3.

Box 1.3   *The self-reference effect: What's in it for me?*

Read the following list of the words aloud to a small group of your friends (Group 1) and ask them to listen carefully while you speak: **Brave**, **humorous**, **mean**, **cold**, **arrogant**, **aggressive**, **sincere**, **confident** and **trustworthy**. Then, about an hour later, ask your friends unexpectedly to write down as many of these words as they can remember. Notice how many words they recall correctly.

Now, repeat the procedure with a different group of friends (Group 2). But this time, tell them that you want them to ask themselves whether or not each of these adjectives applies accurately to their own personalities. As before, test how many words this group can recall when prompted unexpectedly an hour later. Interestingly, what usually happens on this occasion is that Group 2 performs significantly better than Group 1 – suggesting that the act of checking whether something applies to oneself or not helps to improve one's memory. Asking 'what's in it for me?' seems to pay off! It seems that checking for personal relevance helps to glue new material to what we already know or believe. Technically, the self-reference effect may be due to the fact that when people generate their own retrieval cues, these prompts are more powerful than when someone else does so (Sternberg, 1999).

A third benefit of questioning is that it *prepares the mind* for what will follow. Put differently, questions serve as advance organisers for our learning. To explain, research in cognitive psychology suggests that we cannot build an understanding of a series of facts until we have identified a suitable mental scaffolding on which this information may be hung. Therefore, questions help to consolidate the structure of our understanding. Finally, asking questions encourages you to *think critically* because it compels you to distinguish between relevant and irrelevant material in a textbook. Put simply, information is deemed to be relevant if it helps you to answer the particular questions(s) which motivated your study. But it is irrelevant if it has no bearing upon them. For example, if your study question is 'What were the main causes of the French revolution?', then it makes little sense to become side-tracked by events, no matter how interesting, which happened after this era. For all these reasons, writing down your study question before you open your history book allows you to think while you are reading. Therefore, you should never read a book unless you have a pen and paper nearby.

So far in this chapter I've explained that the act of questioning can transform passive or aimless reading into active or deliberate learning. In other words, what makes some people good students is not that they can read rapidly but that they *think* and *question* before they read anything at all. But apart from learning to question what you read, what other academic tasks will you be expected to master in university?

The academic challenges posed by attending university

There are many differences between the academic demands of school and university. To begin with, you will encounter different teaching methods in university (lectures, small-groups/tutorials) from those which you experienced in school. These teaching methods create new demands for you. For example, accurate note-taking at lectures requires you to perform two apparently incompatible skills at the same time – listening and summarising. But as I shall explain in Chapter 4, there are certain tricks of the trade which will help you to become adept at this skill of note-taking. Interestingly, psychologists have also discovered that note-taking becomes easier as you become more confident about what you know. In fact, cognitive researchers argue that *the more you know, the easier it to learn and remember new information* – a principle which we shall return to in Chapter 8. A second new challenge of university comes from the fact that the academic staff there expect you to engage in far more independent reading and study than you did in school. For example, you will be required to consult a number of different sources for your research assignments instead of relying only on your prescribed textbook for the course. But the more books you consult, the more efficient your reading habits must become in order to avoid confusion. Thirdly, as a consequence of this extra reading required in university, you will encounter different criteria of evaluation for your assignments from those which you experienced in school. This discovery may initially prove to be rather disconcerting. For example, you may be shocked to receive a mark of only 50 for a project or essay that would have earned a mark of 85 in school. If this happens to you, then you should seek advice from your lecturer about the specific ways in which your work could be improved. Taken together, the challenges posed by different teaching methods (see also Chapter 9), increased background reading requirements and more abstract assessment criteria are quite significant. In order to find out how well you are prepared for these challenges, please complete the exercise contained in Box 1.4.

Box 1.4	Some learning tasks required in university

Below you will find some learning tasks which are encountered when you study in university. After you have read each one, please indicate whether or not you have ever received any formal training or instruction in it.

Task / skill	Have you ever been trained in it? (y/n)
Motivating myself to study	
Planning and adhering to my study time-tables	
Taking notes in lectures	
Taking notes from books or journals	
Thinking critically about what I hear or read	
Learning how to use the library	
Learning how to concentrate	
Remembering and understanding what I learn	
Researching and writing essays/projects/papers	

As with Box 1.1, if you gave a majority of 'yes' responses to the questions above you are fortunate to be well-prepared for the intellectual demands of university. But if your answers were mostly 'no', then you definitely need some help with your study skills. Ironically, it is precisely those skills in which you received *least* instruction which will influence most strongly your academic success in university. Although there is no single best way of dealing with these challenges (due to the fact that people differ in their learning capacities and preferences), there is a system which will help you to become a more active and independent thinker in university. This system is outlined in the remainder of this book – each chapter being devoted to a separate learning skill.

What makes a successful student?

Research by Hartley (1994) provides a distinctive psychological profile of the study skills of people who are successful in university. Six factors are especially important. First, successful learners are highly motivated to achieve self-set standards of excellence: They do not leave things until the last minute. Second, and not surprisingly, they tend to be well-organised in their work habits (e.g. always adhering to a timetable which has a finishing time as well as a starting time). Third, good students enjoy experimenting with different ways of 'encoding' (taking in) and representing (or storing mentally) course-relevant information (e.g. they revise by making diagrams as well as by reviewing lecture notes). Fourth, they have developed the habit of monitoring their progress – trying to establish links between new information and what they already know. Fifth, they tend to process information at a deeper level than do less successful students. To do this, they try to impose a structure on, or extract relevant principles from, textbook or lecture information. Finally, they recognise the social dimension of learning by seeking regular feedback from academic staff and fellow students. In summary, although most students are prepared for the intellectual demands of university, they find it difficult to achieve an adequate level of self-discipline in their new environment. In other words, they require explicit training in what Goleman (1995) calls 'emotional intelligence'.

Summary

In this chapter I explained some of the main academic demands which you will encounter in university. As most of these tasks (e.g. learning how to take notes and read books efficiently) are predictable, you should relish the challenge which they pose. Ironically, however, the most significant hurdle confronting you – namely, that of managing your own learning – is the one for which you have received *least* formal preparation in school. Accordingly, university is challenging because it requires you to develop not only technical knowledge (e.g. of your chosen academic subjects) but also *meta-cognitive* skills (e.g. the ability to monitor your own concentration while studying). Indeed, your lecturers will assume that you know *how to learn* effectively. Psychologically, the key to effective learning is the art of *posing specific questions* before you read. In other words, effective study depends on thinking clearly before you begin to read at all. So, studying can be defined as a form of deliberate learning in which people search for specific answers to specific questions. The value of this questioning approach to learning is highlighted by the PQRR approach to reading textbook material. As we shall see, this technique advocates previewing the chapter, writing down 2–3 specific study questions, taking notes and reviewing what you have learned. This system is effective because it reminds us that successful students tend to have *questions in search of answers*. That is why they are willing to consult several textbooks with the same questions in mind. On the other hand, unsuccessful students tend to change their questions to suit the book which they happen to be reading. Clearly, this form of learning is both passive and accidental. Overall, the main theme of this chapter is the idea that you have to take personal responsibility for becoming an active learner in university. Asking questions is the first step in this journey.

2. Getting Down to Study: Motivating Yourself and Developing a Habit of Learning

Introduction

Have you ever experienced an irresistible urge to tidy your room, make a phone call or have yet another cup of coffee when you're faced with the task of reading a textbook or working on an academic assignment? If so, then you have allowed displacement activities (or self-created distractions) to give you an excuse for not getting down to academic work. But you are not unique in this regard. Overcoming inertia is a constant battle for anyone faced with an ill-defined and time-consuming task such as studying or writing. After all, very few people wake up thinking 'I *really* feel like studying today!' But just because you're rarely in the mood to study does not mean that you cannot train yourself to work in a determined and efficient manner. In fact, as the famous psychologist William James observed over a century ago, 'it's easier to act your way into a feeling than to feel your way into action'. In other words, our behaviour often determines our mood – not the other way around. Mindful of this idea, the novelist Peter De Vries once remarked that 'I write when I'm inspired – but I see to it that I'm inspired at nine o'clock every morning!' Clearly, establishing a strict work routine is one antidote to lethargy. But what other techniques can you use tó motivate yourself to get down to study? The purpose of this chapter is to provide some practical answers to this question. Briefly, I shall explain three ways in which you can increase your motivation to study. First, you can use self-administered rewards (positive reinforcement) to strengthen your study habits. Second, you can use goal-setting principles to establish specific, challenging and measurable targets for your learning. Finally, you can develop a consistent habit of learning by re-organising your study environment and by establishing study routines.

This chapter is organised as follows. First, I shall help you to understand your motivation in attending university. Next, I shall explore the nature, types and origins of motivation in your academic life. Finally, I shall explain three ways in which you can increase your motivation to study. As I said, these motivational techniques include the use of rewards, the application of goal-setting procedures and the re-organisation of your learning environment and habits.

Assessing your motivation to study

Why did you come to university? In order to explore this question, please try the exercise in Box 2.1.

Box 2.1 *Exploring your motivation to attend university*

Please read each of the statements below and then indicate your level of agreement with it by using a five-point rating scale, where 1= 'does not apply to me at all' and 5 = 'is very accurate'. To benefit from this exercise, you must be completely honest in your views. There are no right or wrong answers. It is *your* views alone which matter.

I came to university because . . .

Rating

1. *I wanted to improve my education in a specific field*
2. *My parents / family put pressure on me to go there*
3. *I wanted to develop and mature as a person*
4. *It fills in the time for me until I know what I want to do*
5. *It provides a great opportunity to learn new things*
6. *I wanted to get away from home*
7. *I liked the idea of being free for a few years more*
8. *I didn't want to waste my Leaving Certificate points*
9. *A university degree is a sign of achievement for me*
10. *The career I wish to pursue requires a university degree*

Have you answered all of the questions? If so, can you detect any pattern in your responses? Notice that statements 2, 4, 6, 7 and 8 reflect a passive orientation or externally-motivated reasons for going to university whereas statements 1, 3, 5, 9 and 10 reflect a more self-motivated and 'internal' approach.

It is important to clarify your reasons for attending university because they provide the motivational foundation on which your studies will be built. Indeed, motivational factors play a significant role in determining academic success in university. To explain, the selection test for entry to university assesses ability more than motivation. In other words, incoming university students are selected more on intellectual than on motivational grounds. Accordingly, these students tend to vary from each other more in motivation than in intellectual ability. But as the challenge of managing one's own learning (see Chapter 1) demands discipline and perseverance rather than academic knowledge, motivation proves to be a crucial determinant of university degree results. This point is echoed by American psychologist Martin Seligman who argues that 'What's missing in tests of ability is *motivation*. What you need to know about someone is whether they will keep going when things get frustrating. My hunch is that for a given level of intelligence, your actual achievement is a function not just of talent, but also of the capacity to stand defeat' (cited in Goleman, 1995, p. 89, italics mine).

What is motivation?

Derived from the Latin word *movere* (meaning to move), motivation is concerned with all the factors which initiate, direct and sustain our behaviour. Accordingly, a motive is a want or a need that moves us to act in certain ways. For example, we might want to study a topic because we find it fascinating in itself (intrinsic motivation) or simply because it has to be covered for an impending examination (extrinsic motivation).

Motivation plays a vital role in determining success in any field. For example, Ericsson (1996) found that people such as Olympic athletes, world-class musicians and chess grand-masters share a remarkable ability to pursue a relentless programme of training activities, whether or not they feel like doing it. In fact, by the age of 20, these people have clocked up an estimated 20,000 hours of dedicated practice in their chosen field. Similarly, Howe's (1999) analysis of the lives of creative people (e.g. Darwin, Einstein) led him to conclude that genius is not a 'gift' but the product of a remarkable mixture of practice and perseverance. But apart from showing more commitment than others, experts in any field tend to *think* differently from less successful counterparts as well. To illustrate, consider how students differ from each other in the way in which they account for their everyday successes and failures. Most people tend to attribute their successes (e.g. passing an exam) to their own abilities and their failures to transient environmental factors (e.g. bad luck). This optimistic explanatory style sustains motivation because it encourages people to believe that they have the ability to overcome any temporary setbacks which they encounter. Conversely, students with a pessimistic explanatory style tend to attribute their successes to environmental factors (e.g. luck) but their *failures* to *internal* factors such as lack of intelligence. Clearly, pessimists have trouble in motivating themselves because they do not think that they have sufficient ability to do well academically. This finding has been neatly summarised by Zimbardo, Weber & Johnson (2000) who said that optimists can't lose and pessimists can't win – regardless of what academic results they achieve!

Types of motivation

We can distinguish between two types of motives: primary (biological) and secondary (psychological). Primary motives consist of instinctive needs which must be satisfied in order to keep us alive. For example, hunger, thirst and a need for shelter and warmth fall into this category. Conversely, secondary motives are learned desires which, although not linked directly to our biological survival, influence our happiness and well-being. For example, most people have a desire to socialise with other people (affiliation motivation). Also, they strive to attain success in some area (e.g. school, sport, business) of their lives (a phenomenon called achievement motivation). In practice, these two categories of needs overlap considerably in everyday life. To illustrate, consider the following situation.

Imagine that you are studying so diligently in the library for an imminent examination that you forget to take a lunch-break. After a while, your stomach starts to rumble and you begin to feel so hungry that you find yourself thinking of food. This thought is very distracting and you begin to feel restless. In fact, you discover that you've been staring at the page for the last few minutes, reading the same sentence in your textbook over and over again (a signal that you have lost your concentration; see Chapter 6). At this point, you decide to take action. So, you walk out of the library and over to the restaurant for a snack. Unfortunately, as it's late, you discover that the restaurant is now closed. However, you suddenly remember that the university bar is open. And there, you bump into some friends and have a cup of coffee and a sandwich with them. You haven't seen them for a while so there is a lot to talk about. But after half an hour, you begin to feel uneasy again and you tell your friends that it's time to return to your books. Ignoring their pleas to stay for a drink, you tell them about your forthcoming examination and walk briskly back to the library. When you sit down, you feel refreshed and eager to get back to work.

In this vignette, several motives shaped your behaviour. To begin with, your departure from the library, and subsequent visits to the restaurant and bar, were initiated in the attempt to satisfy the primary need of hunger. But once your snack was over, another motivational conflict was precipitated. Would you sit down with your friends or go back to your studies? This clash between your affiliation and achievement needs is interesting for two reasons. First, it reveals how, in many everyday situations, your behaviour can be pushed and pulled in different directions. To explain, whereas you may have felt that you were being pushed by your friends into staying with them in the bar, you felt pulled to the library as a result of your desire to do well in an examination. Clearly, on this occasion, your motivation to study outweighed your desire to socialise. But it's rarely that simple. You may find yourself sitting in the library but thinking about the fun you're missing in the bar. Of course, this approach-avoidance conflict can be minimised by learning to associate certain places with study – a strategy I shall return to later in the chapter. But there is a second reason why this conflict between motives is instructive. Specifically, it shows us that when two motives clash, a good solution may be to defer the satisfaction of one of them. And it is this capacity to defer gratification which is an important component of our emotional intelligence (e.g. Goleman, 1995) or our ability to regulate our feelings so that we can behave more effectively in everyday life. So, the fact that you know that you can meet your friends again means that you can postpone satisfaction of your need to affiliate with other people. But the fact that your examination is imminent should convince you to increase the priority of your study behaviour. In summary, our motivation *to do anything* is always influenced by a subtle blend of internal and external factors. Let us explore some of these factors now.

Sources of motivation

As I explained in Box 2.1 (p. 15), our motivation can come from either internal or external factors. Internal motivation (or push) refers to a desire to perform a task *for its own sake* rather than for any obvious external rewards which it might yield. For example, people who spend a long time engaging in their hobbies typify this form of motivation. Interestingly, it is this intrinsic satisfaction which characterises the motivation of many successful performers. To illustrate, consider the importance which the Australian swimmer Kieren Perkins, who won a gold medal in the 1992 Olympics, attached to intrinsic motivation: 'I always *race against myself to improve my own perfor-mances*. The fact that I sometimes set world records in the process is a bonus. My personal best performance is the goal, not necessarily the world record' (cited in Morris & Summers, 1995, italics mine). Similarly, the brilliant golfer Tiger Woods revealed that his main motivation sprang from enjoying the challenge of beating his own personal record (Scott, 1999). In contrast, external motivation (or pull) refers to a desire to do something mainly because it provides certain rewarding consequences. For example, some students regard a degree purely and simply as a means to an end. What motivates them in university is not the intrinsic challenge of acquiring new skills and knowledge but the external prospect of getting a well-paid job after graduation.

Increasing your motivation

As I explained earlier, there are at least three practical ways of increasing your motivation. First, you can use self-administered rewards to shape the desired behaviour. Second, you can motivate yourself through effective goal-setting. Finally, you can re-design your study environ-ment so that it becomes a more enticing place in which to work.

Using rewards to strengthen your behaviour: The power of positive reinforcement

About a century ago, an American psychologist called Edward Lee Thorndike conducted a series of experiments in which he studied the problem-solving behaviour of captive animals. In particular, he analysed how cats tried to escape from puzzle-boxes by locating special bars or bolts which, when pressed, would open the doors of the cages and lead to a reward of food. Thorndike found that rewards changed the initially random behaviour of the cats in a significant way. Specifically, when cats who had managed to escape from their cages were put back into them, they quickly searched for the release mechanism that had worked previously. This finding led Thorndike to conclude that any behaviour which is rewarded will be strengthened and hence become more likely in the future – a principle known as the 'law of effect'. Influenced by Thorndike's view that environmental consequences influenced the actions that preceded them, another famous psychologist called B.F. Skinner delved deeper into the way in which rewards and punishments influence our behaviour. In particular, he showed that whereas positive reinforcers (whether tangible rewards such as food or intangible rewards like compliments) tend to strengthen associated behaviour, punishment (e.g. receiving a low grade or criticism from a teacher) tends to dampen behaviour. So, how can you apply this principle of reinforcement to increase your motivation to study? The answer is: by rewarding yourself for successful study behaviour.

A key principle in learning theory is the idea that activities which are followed by rewards gradually tend to become rewarding *in themselves*. In other words, if you learn to associate studying with pleasurable consequences, then, over time, studying will become an enjoyable activity on its own. To apply this principle, you should begin to give yourself specific rewards (e.g. watching television, having a coffee break, going for a walk, visiting a friend) for accomplishing planned study goals (e.g. to summarise a designated chapter in your textbook). Of course, for this system to work, you must make sure to reward yourself only for the 'right' actions – achieving study targets. Otherwise you may inadvertently strengthen undesirable behaviour and slipshod work habits. For example, if you take a break every time you encounter a difficult topic in your studies (the 'I'll get back to that later' philosophy), then you are encouraging *avoidance* rather than persistence. So, remember the rule: reward yourself for work done – not work avoided. Interestingly, the fact that rewards increase motivation means that you don't have to be *initially* interested in something in order to study it thoroughly. By breaking an assignment into stepping stones, and by rewarding yourself for achieving each target along the way, you can learn to motivate yourself indefinitely. But apart from using self-administered rewards, how else can you increase your motivation to study? The answer lies in a technique called goal-setting.

Increasing your motivation through goal-setting:
Study SMARTer, not harder

In Chapter 1, I suggested that reading without a question in mind was like driving a car around in circles. The engine is working perfectly – but you're not actually going anywhere. By analogy, effective motivation requires *direction* as well as drive. And such motivation can be enhanced by a technique called goal-setting.

A goal is a target or objective which we strive to attain (e.g. passing an exam or submitting an assignment on time). Accordingly, goal-setting is the process by which we set targets for ourselves. Interestingly, research shows that some types of targets are better motivators than others. For example, goals which are specific (e.g. reading a particular chapter in a named book) and under our control (e.g. to devise study questions before we read a chapter) tend to elicit greater effort and persistence than do more general targets (e.g. to 'read around the course'). To learn more about effective goal-setting, please consult Box 2.2.

Box 2.2   *Principles of goal-setting*

To be effective, goal-setting should follow certain principles. These principles are best explained by using the acronym SMART (Bull, Albinson & Shambrook, 1996). Briefly, each letter of this acronym stands for a different feature of an effective goal.

S = specific
The clearer and more specific your goal is, the more likely you are to achieve it. For example, a goal such as 'I want to make notes on Chapter 8 of my Chemistry textbook tonight between 7 p.m. and 8 p.m.' is more motivating than 'I may do some Chemistry later if I have time'.

M = measurable
If you cannot measure your progress towards your goal, then you will quickly lose interest in it. So it is useful to keep a record of your progress. For example, if you're drafting a paper on computer, you could use the 'word count' command to record the number of words you've written every night – just to remind yourself that you're making steady progress on the task.

A = action-related
Unless you identify a number of action steps (tasks which take you a step nearer to your goal and which involve specific actions that are under your control) for each of your study goals, you may feel confused about what to do next. For example, after each lecture you attend, you should ask yourself: what specific books can I look up in the library in order to learn more about this topic?

R = realistic
Your study goals should be realistic and achievable using the resources available to you. Therefore, it is vital to discuss the feasibility of your goals with relevant academic staff (especially when you are working relatively independently of your supervisor e.g. in project assignments, see Chapter 9).

T = time-based
Have you ever noticed that most people do not begin jobs until a deadline approaches? Clearly, time-pressures create a sense of urgency which motivates us. But to avoid the panic which such pressure can cause, it is best to *work backwards* from the completion date to the present date. For example, tell yourself: 'In order to submit the assignment by the end of next month, I shall have to have it written by the middle of the month, which means I shall have to do the background research for it by next week'.

In general, goal-setting works best when you work systematically through each of the following steps.

Step 1   Identify your goals
Write down a list of *three study goals*. These goals should be under your control and as specific as possible. Write them down as promises to yourself or affirmation statements. For example, 'Today, between 7 p.m. and 7. 50 p.m., I shall look for an answer to the following question . . .'.

Step 2   Establish priorities
The next step involves ranking these goals in terms of priority. Put a '1' beside the goal which you feel is most important at present, a '2' beside the next most important and a '3' beside the least important goal.

Step 3   Consider a time-scale
Classify your goals into three columns depending on the time-frame involved: long-term (e.g. for the end of the year), intermediate (for the end of the semester) and short-term (for this week).

Step 4   Break the goal into action-steps
Next, break up each of your goals into specific action-steps (i.e. things which you can do which will help you to get closer to one of your goals). For example, if one of your goals was 'to evaluate the novel *Pride and Prejudice* by the end of next week', then obvious action steps are to obtain and read the novel and to consult the library for at least two critical commentaries on this novel.

Step 5   Review your progress
To benefit maximally from goal-setting, you must build a review process into your work. One way to do this is to use some time

(perhaps even half an hour) at the end of every week in order to check how far away you are from achieving your goals for that week.

Step 6 Revise your goals if necessary
Flexibility is a key feature of the goal-setting cycle. Be prepared to revise your goals if you are pressed for time.

Organising your environment and your routines

Learning is not just something which happens in one's head. It invariably involves a change in *behaviour* as well as increased knowledge. In other words, learning involves *doing* things as well as gathering more information. So in this section, I shall provide some practical tips on how to develop the behavioural habit of learning efficiently. As we shall see, this task involves at least five steps. First, you should find a quiet room or location which you can transform into your personal work environment. Second, you need to establish a regular study period throughout the week. Third, you should have a specific purpose in mind otherwise you will end up daydreaming (see also Chapter 6). Fourth, you must learn to use rewards in order to sustain your motivation in performing study tasks that may not initially appear interesting to you. Finally, you will benefit from learning how to *finish* a study session by leaving your work in such a way as to entice you to begin it again enthusiastically the next time. By the way, Chapter 3 extends this analysis of learning habits by explaining how you can manage your study time as efficiently as possible.

Find a quiet location
Finding a place in which you *know* that you will be able to study (your personal work environment) is vital to your learning habit. If you keep varying the place in which you study, you are acting like someone who tries to start his or her car with a different set of keys each time. Remember that just as only one key fits your ignition, so also will only one place be associated in your mind with learning. So, what are the requirements of this place? The ideal room in which to study should have the following characteristics: adequate space (so that you can sit comfortably at your desk or table); a clear work-top which is sufficiently large to allow you to spread out the books and notes that you are currently working on; a comfortable, straight-backed chair; storage space or shelving near the desk; natural light, where possible, and, of course, plenty of peace and quiet. In summary, it is essential to find a warm, quiet, reasonably spacious, well-illuminated and distraction-free place in which to study.

If you intend to work at home, then you should make sure that you have a desk or table, a straight-backed chair, a good lamp and plenty of pens and paper at hand. By studying in this place regularly, you will condition yourself (see p. 19) to work in it. As a result of this conditioning, you will find that you can learn to concentrate as soon as you sit down at your desk or table. You will switch on your mental ignition quickly and reduce the typical settling-in time that you would experience if you continued to vary your work location.

Although most quiet, well-lit locations make suitable places of study, a word of caution should be offered about trying to study in bed or while lying down on a sofa. The problem with these situations or postures is that they are passive, relaxing and likely to encourage you to daydream or to fall asleep. Indeed, it is possible that falling asleep over your textbooks is a habit that could generalise to library contexts quite easily! And speaking of the library, if you wish to study there, it is a good idea to choose an isolated location far away from the stairs or door. Otherwise, you'll be tempted to interrupt your own studies by glancing repeatedly at people who pass by.

Regardless of where it is located, your study environment should have sufficient desk space available to enable you to spread your books and notes out in front of you. Thus when you sit down to study, it is helpful to have pens, paper and all your relevant books or notes within easy reach. The idea here is that if you have to get up repeatedly to look for your study material, your concentration will be broken. Therefore, all likely sources of distraction (e.g. television, photographs) should be kept out of reach and out of your eye line.

How to study in noisy environments

So far, I've indicated some factors which characterise ideal study environments. But what if you can't find one? What happens if you have to study in crowded libraries or in noisy houses? Also, is it possible to do any constructive work while you commute to and from university? There are two main strategies for getting the most out of a distracting study environment. First, you have to prepare properly. This involves reducing your books and notes to a bare minimum so that your mind can focus on only one academic task at a time. Second, try to be as active as possible in such environments by taking notes carefully and by checking regularly on what you have written. This advice about coping with distractions brings us to an important practical issue for many students: does background music or noise affect the efficiency of study? To find out, read Box 2.3.

Establish a regular study time

Most people have developed a regular pattern in their lives. For example, you probably go to bed at around the same time on most week-nights and, as likely as not, you tend to sit in the same place in your lecture theatres during term. In view of these daily habits which we form quite easily, it is not surprising that we should consider establishing a regular period of study time for ourselves. It doesn't matter much at what time of the day this study period is scheduled for although the 'state dependency' principle of learning (see Box 2.3) suggests that the closer your study time matches your examination time, the better prepared you will be for the examination itself. However, regardless of the precise time involved, what is vital is that your study schedule should be repeated regularly during the week. In other words, you should try as much as possible to study in the same place at the same time every day or evening. A useful tip in this regard is to visualise this study period of the night as 'red traffic time' which, like a red traffic light, gives you the signal to stop all other activities while you study. Conversely, other periods of the day could be pictured as 'green traffic time' during which you can meet friends, watch television or get on with mundane chores. A detailed discussion of practical strategies for effective time management is provided in Chapter 3.

Have a specific purpose in mind

In Chapter 1, I explained the importance of questioning in active learning. Therefore, you should develop the habit of writing down 2–3 specific study questions before you begin your reading. To remind yourself of your goal, 'ink it, don't think it' (see also Chapter 5).

Start with a simple lead in task

Have you ever noticed how difficult it is to settle down to studying? It's as if your mind knows that it will be expected to work hard and is looking for an excuse to withdraw. A good way of overcoming this problem of inertia and restlessness is to try to schedule your studies so that you start with a simple lead-in task (e.g. glancing through the summary of a chapter without taking any notes). There is a great deal of psychological truth in the Irish saying that *'tosach maith, leath na h-oibre!'* ('a good start is half the battle').

Finish your study by preparing for the next time

A subtle trick in building your learning habit is to leave your work environment as inviting as possible so that you will start enthusiastically the next time you get down to study (Butler & Hope, 1995). The

| Box 2.3 | *The effects of background music on studying* |

'Turn it down – how can you possibly study with that noise on?' For years, exasperated parents have challenged their children about the feasibility of studying effectively while listening to background music. Their argument is that students will not be able to concentrate properly if they are dividing their attention between their books and the music in the background. After all, you can only listen to one thing at a time – can't you? In reply, however, most students are equally convinced that pleasant or relaxing background music can actually *improve* their concentration. Which of these arguments is correct? Well, psychological research tends to favour the parental position – but *not* their theoretical explanation. To explain, the principle of 'state dependency of learning' suggests that one of the best ways to recall something which happened in the past is to re-create the actual conditions under which the original learning occurred. The closer the resemblance between the learning and testing conditions, the greater are the chances of accurate recall. As an application of this principle, police authorities may re-construct crime scenes in order to jog people's memories for details which may have been blocked out until they were in the same situation again. Interestingly, this idea of state dependency applies to psychological states as much as to physical environments. For example, when people are depressed, their memories tend to focus selectively on equally bleak experiences in the past. Accordingly, it can be difficult to get people to snap out of a depressed mood. But how does this research relate to the impact of background music on studying? Put simply, it seems that background music does not affect what goes into people's minds (especially if they can control the volume of such sound) but it does affect the conditions under which it comes *out* of the mind best. In other words, background music is more likely to affect memory than concentration because examinations are done in silence. And according to the state dependency principle, students would have to re-create the background music to simulate their habitual learning environment. Naturally, such an arrangement is impossible in an examination. Can you imagine an invigilator seeking background musical or television requests as students file into an examination hall? To summarise, it is not advisable to study while you listen to background music simply because it is poor preparation for the task of recalling what you learned in the silence of an examination.

*Develop a learning habit by studying at the
same time in the same place every day*

problem with most students is that they are so anxious to finish studying that they leave their books and notes in a state of disarray. Obviously, such a sight is very demoralising when you have to study that material again. So, it may be a good idea to spend the last 2–3 minutes of your study schedule in tidying your books and notes – perhaps even writing down some specific study questions which need to be addressed when you resume your work.

Summary

Most students find it difficult to get down to study. And even when they conquer this inertia, a host of irrelevant tasks (or displacement activities such as taking a break or making a phone call) may prove to be irresistible. Clearly, motivational problems are a powerful impediment to learning for people of all ages and abilities. Therefore, the purpose of this chapter was to explore what motivation is, where it comes from and how to harness it properly to develop an efficient habit of learning. As I explained, the term motivation refers to all those factors which initiate, direct and sustain our behaviour. To begin with, I helped you to clarify your motives for attending university in the first place. As you discovered, these motives reflect a blend of external and internal factors. For example, going to university because of perceived parental pressure suggests an external source of motivation, whereas wanting to improve your education for personal reasons indicates an internal achievement orientation. Although both kinds of factors may drive your studies equally well, self-motivation is more important than external influences in the long run as it encourages persistence in times of difficulty. But effective study requires *direction* as well as drive or energy. Therefore, in the remainder of the chapter, I explained three practical motivational techniques which can improve the quality of your learning by directing it along desired lines. First, I showed you how to use rewards to strengthen your study behaviour. A key principle here is that activities which are followed by rewarding consequences tend to become rewarding in themselves. Next, using goal-setting principles, I explained how to study SMARTer rather than harder. To explain, the acronym SMART represents the first letters of the qualities which study goals should have if they are to elicit optimal motivation. These qualities are **s**pecific, **m**easurable, **a**ction-related, **r**ealistic and **t**ime-based. Finally, I explained how a reorganisation of your study environment and behavioural routines can improve the quality of your learning. This section also included a discussion of the effects of background music on studying. As I indicated, such music does not normally affect the information which goes *into* your mind – but it can determine the circumstances under which this information comes *out* of your mind (i.e. recall conditions). Therefore, you should study in silence simply because you will be tested under silent conditions in the exam-hall.

3. Managing Your Study Time Effectively: How Much? How Often? For How Long?

'I wasted time and now doth time waste me' (Shakespeare, *King Richard II, V.v*)

'Never put off until tomorrow what you can avoid altogether!' (students' graffiti)

'A small daily task, if it be really daily, will beat the labours of a spasmodic Hercules' (Anthony Trollope)

'Má chaillean tú uair ar maidin beidh tú á tóraiocht i rith an lae'
(If you lose an hour in the morning you will be looking for it all day)

Introduction

Many people believe that there is a direct relationship between study time and academic success. In other words, the more time you spend studying, the better you will do in examinations. Unfortunately, this theory is misleading for two reasons. First, you can sit in front of your books for hours and yet achieve nothing because of a tendency to daydream (see also Chapter 6). In addition, research shows that it is the *quality* rather than the quantity of your study that determines the richness of your learning. For example, a duration of two hours spent in seeking specific answers to specific questions (see Chapter 5) is more beneficial than is a period of *four* hours spent in passive transcription from a textbook. Similarly, transcribing lecture notes to make them neater is more wasteful of time than is trying to summarise the key points that they contain. Bearing these ideas in mind, a significant challenge for you as a student is to learn some effective time-management skills. Indeed, there is evidence that over 40 per cent of first-year students worry about their use of study time (Moran *et al.*, 1991). This result is not surprising when the demands of university are compared with those of school. For example, the number of hours that university students spend in class is much smaller than that which they are expected to use for the purpose of private study. The implication of this finding is simple: without proper training, your free time in university can easily become wasted time. Therefore, the purpose of the present chapter is to provide some practical advice on getting maximum benefit from your study time. For example, how *long* should your study sessions last? And how *often* should you study?

In an effort to answer these time-management questions, this chapter is organised as follows. To begin with, I shall help you to assess your current use of study time. Then I shall explore the main time-wasters which may hamper your studies at present and suggest some ways of overcoming them. Finally, I shall explain some practical time-management techniques ranging from daily goal-setting to making effective timetables. This section will also feature a discussion of the merits of 'spaced' versus 'massed' learning (the latter being known more popularly as cramming).

Assessing your use of study time

How do you spend your time in university on a typical day during term? In order to answer this question, please complete the Activity Diary exercise in Box 3.1.

Why do we waste study time?

Wasting study time means spending it unwisely on activities which you *know* to be irrelevant to your academic goals. For example, playing arcade games when you should be at lectures is pointless. But working in a part-time job to pay for books or other university expenses is not a waste of time. Similarly, you should not feel guilty about socialising with your friends after a good day's work. But no matter how firm your resolve is, you will encounter numerous situations in university which challenge your time-management skills to the limit. Some of these time-wasting situations are described below. Which of them can you identify with and how can you overcome them?

Lacking a clear focus: Not knowing how or where to start
Reading without any clear idea of what you are looking for is a waste of time. So also is feeling sorry for yourself because nobody has told you where to start or what to study. This latter problem stems from the fact that academic courses in university are relatively unstructured and demand unspecified amounts of background reading. But instead of worrying about this problem, you can tackle it as follows.

Box 3.1   *My activity diary: Charting my use of time*

Pick a recent day during term (e.g. yesterday). Then fill in brief details of your time log under the two columns indicated: what academic activity you engaged in (e.g. attending a lecture, looking for a book in the library) and whether or not this activity was planned.

Time period	The day in question	
	Academic activity	*Was it planned or spontaneous?*
9.30 – 10.30		
10.30 – 11.30		
11.30 – 12.30		
14.00 – 15.00		
15.00 – 16.00		
16.00 – 17.00		
19.00 – 20.00		
20.00 – 21.00		

Is any trend evident with regard to your use of study time for the day in question? Were the majority of your academic activities planned or unplanned on that day? By examining the pattern of your activity diary, you may discover that you had a lot more time available for private study than you had realised. Also, you may discover that your learning is influenced more by accidental than by deliberate factors (see also Chapter 1) – a typical sign that you need to cultivate some time-management skills.

First, you must try to *impose some structure* on the syllabus so that you can identify your priorities and plan to distribute your time accordingly. This can be achieved by seeking advice from your tutors and lecturers (during their office hours) about the relative importance of different topics on the course. How can you know what is important and what to focus on unless you *ask* someone? Second, as I have explained elsewhere (see Chapter 1 and Chapter 5), you should write down 2–3 *specific study questions* before you begin to read a textbook.

Procrastination

Even when we know exactly what we have to study, we tend to procrastinate by finding reasons for postponing our work indefinitely. For example, do any of the following excuses sound familiar to you?

> 'I work better under pressure'
> 'I'm not in the right mood for it at the moment'
> 'I'll get around to it later'
> 'The weather is so hot/cold that I can't study properly'
> 'I'll do it after I've watched television'

If so, then you're an accomplished procrastinator! But remember that if something is important to you, you'll *make* time for it *right now.* Remember the old phrase, 'one of these days is none of these days'. But how can you focus on the present? One solution is to say to yourself 'I'll make a start' and break up your study task into smaller components, taking one step at a time. Also, you could use the idea from Chapter 2 that mood follows action. In other words, actually working on something gets you into the right frame of mind to continue the job.

Task hopping

The habit of jumping from one study activity to another depending on your prevailing mood is a symptom of poor concentration and inefficient time-management. As I shall explain in Chapter 6, you can train your mind to focus on one job at a time by using such techniques as goal-setting and routine preparation.

Travelling to and from university

Most students dismiss the hours they spend in commuting to and from university as dead time. But travel time can be used fruitfully if you use it to glance over summary sheets which contain condensed answers to typical questions asked in exams (see also revision techniques in Chapter 10).

In summary, time-wasters can come in many different guises. What they have in common is the fact that they have the capacity to divert your attention away from what is important and towards what is irrelevant to your academic concerns. The best way to overcome them is by renewing your commitment every day (see Box 3.2) and by using a set of practical time-management techniques which are described in the next section.

Box 3.2 *No more excuses: Making a promise to yourself*

Having identified some common time-wasters, try to pick the one which afflicts you most frequently. Then write a simple promise to yourself indicating how you are going to overcome this problem right now. For example, 'Before I go to the library this afternoon, I'm going to write down three specific study questions which will guide my work there'.

Techniques for managing your study time effectively

According to Butler & Hope (1995), successful time-management boils down to 'doing those things you value or those things that help you achieve your goals' (p. 32). Unfortunately, this advice assumes that you have already established your study goals and priorities. But if you're like most students, you have probably drifted through university without planning specific academic goals. If so, then you could benefit from the following time-management techniques.

Daily goal-setting

In Chapter 2, I explained the SMART approach to goal-setting. This approach encourages you to set goals for your study which are specific, measurable, action-related, realistic and time-based. By using this technique, you will learn to stop wasting time in pursuit of goals which are outside your control (e.g. getting first place in your class at the end of the year) and start to work on targets which are *immediate* and *within your control* (e.g. asking questions of your lecturer after class or reading a specific chapter in your textbook at a designated time). Clearly, spending five minutes every morning writing down your specific study goals for that day will give you a sense of purpose that will insulate you against distractions. Another reason why daily goal-setting is helpful is that immediate targets are more motivating than more distant objectives. If you plan for the present, the future will look after itself (see also Chapter 6). As described in Box 3.2, you should write down your goals as promises or 'affirmation statements' – intentions that are expressed in the first person. For example, 'Tonight, between 7 p.m. and 7.50 p.m., I shall look for an answer to the following question. . .'.

Establish daily study priorities

The best way to establish your study priorities is to distinguish between three kinds of study tasks: 'jobs I *must do* today' (high priority tasks such as attending lectures); 'jobs I *should do* today' (desirable but not essential on a daily basis e.g. studying in the library); and 'jobs I'd *like to do* today' (e.g. to read 'around' the course). Your 'must do tasks' should become top priorities in your *Daily Job List* for university.

Develop routines

Establish a routine for lecture and non-lecture days. First, make a job list. Then, for 2–3 minutes try to anticipate in your imagination the lectures you will attend. For example, you could ask yourself questions such as: Who is the lecturer? What course is it? What did s/he cover last week? What will s/he explore this week? Afterwards, you could spend 2–3 minutes going through a brief after-lecture routine (e.g. Have I attached my lecture notes to the previous lecture on this course? What specific books/articles did the lecturer mention? If I did not note them, can I get this information from a classmate?).

Study briefly and regularly: Distribute your time efficiently

As I mentioned at the beginning of this chapter, research suggests that people learn better if they study for short periods frequently (distributed study) than for long periods infrequently (cramming). Scheduling your study time in short but regular blocks has several advantages. First, it means that you will receive a steady diet of success every day. In addition, it will allow you to remain alert and focused over your books. Finally, during the time between your study sessions, your mind may benefit from a process called incubation whereby new ideas settle in or become consolidated in your mind. This principle of distributed learning is explained in detail in Box 3.3.

Box 3.3 *Massed versus distributed study: Why cramming is ineffective*

It has long been known that the more you study something, the more likely you will be to remember it. But it was not until the late 1880s that the German psychologist Hermann Ebbinghaus discovered that the way in which we *allocate* or *distribute* our study time over a given period is a critical factor in determining how much learning occurs. In particular, it is more beneficial to spread your study over several occasions (distributed or spaced practice) than it is to cram everything into one session (massed practice). As he put it, 'with any considerable number of repetitions, a suitable distribution of them over a space of time is decidedly more advantageous than the massing of them at a single time' (Ebbinghaus, 1885/1964, p. 89). By implication, students who distribute their study sessions over a week (e.g. engaging in one hour of work per night) do better than those who study for the same number of hours at one stretch (Searleman & Herrmann, 1994).

A good illustration of the beneficial effects of distributed practice comes from a study by Bahrick & Phelps (1987). These researchers initially taught people to learn Spanish vocabulary words either distributed over a period of 30 days or all on a single day. Testing these people eight years later, the authors found that the 30-day spaced learning group recalled twice as many Spanish words correctly as did the group who had engaged only in cramming. The practical implication of this research is that it is more beneficial to study for six separate periods of one hour each than for a single intensive period of six hours in duration. As Sternberg (1999) suggests, you will probably recall information better and longer if you distribute your learning over regular study periods instead of trying to cram it all at once. Cramming was also criticised by William James (1890) who observed that

things learned in a few hours, on one occasion, for one purpose, cannot possibly have formed many associations with other things in the mind ... Speedy oblivion is the almost inevitable fate of all that is committed to memory in this simple way . . . Whereas on the contrary, the same information taken in gradually, day after day, recurring in different contexts, . . . and repeatedly reflected on, grow into a fabric, lie open to so many paths of approach, that they remain as permanent possessions (1890/1950, Vol. 1, p. 663).

Why does spaced learning work so well? There are several possible explanations. First, when people engage in cramming, their concentration tends to waver as they get tired so that the actual time they spend at their desks is not a good index of the amount of mental work they have accomplished. A second explanation for the beneficial effect of distributed learning concerns 'encoding processes' (see Chapter 8). Each time a person sits down to study in the short sessions, the context for encoding the information may vary – thereby encouraging the learners to develop richer and more elaborate schemas to understand the material. In other words, each time we think of something, we may make an additional memory trace of it. Therefore, the more memory traces that have been generated, the greater is our likelihood of recalling the information later. A third explanation is that the more opportunities that a person has to expand or augment what s/he is learning, the more understandable it becomes (a form of elaborative rehearsal).

Unfortunately, some cramming is inevitable in university. For example, if there is little time left before an examination and one has not studied at all, then cramming may be the only course of action left. Also, if the interval between the study sessions in a distributed practice schedule is random or too great, forgetting may occur. However, there is one major reason why cramming is a dangerous activity. To explain, staying up late before examinations can make students tired and can cause exam blank in which they experience the awful feeling of knowing that they know something but being unable to recall it at that moment.

How much study? For how long ?

Academics are often asked to advise students on how much study to conduct in university. Unfortunately, to paraphrase George Bernard Shaw, 'the golden rule is that there is *no* golden rule!'. As courses differ widely in their demands, and as students differ so much in their interests and abilities, it is impossible to offer significant conclusions about the optimal amount or duration of study required for academic success. As a rule of thumb, however, it is conventional to recommend scheduling at least *two hours of private study for each hour of formal lectures* on your timetable. This two-hour period should be used as follows:

- To maximise your concentration, study in blocks of 40–50 minutes

- Specify at least one study question per 40-minute block

- After two hours, spend five minutes reviewing what you learned (see principle of 'overlearning' in Chapter 8)

- Acknowledge any persistent distractions that occur by noting them on a 'distraction list' which you can deal with after your study session

- Look for opportunities, of 5–10 minutes duration each day (e.g. between lectures, while waiting for a friend, while travelling in a bus or train) to quickly scan your 'summary sheets' (see Chapter 10)

It's better to study regularly and briefly
than to cram at the last minute

• Use spare moments to revise or to plan. There is bound to be free time even in the busiest of academic timetables. For example, you might find that you have an hour to spend in between scheduled lectures. In this case, you could either review what you learned in the previous lecture or check your progress on your daily job list.

Distinguish between urgent and important tasks

Experts on time-management make a distinction between two kinds of tasks. On the one hand, urgent jobs are tasks (e.g. to submit a paper as part of your course-work) which have to be completed by a certain deadline. On the other hand, important tasks are those which have a clear and specific relevance to your personal study-goals. For example, if you are interested in a particular career such as marketing, then it may be important for you to arrange work experience for the summer in the marketing department of a company at home or abroad. Planning, obtaining relevant information and making personal contacts in this field are important but not necessarily urgent goals. And yet, these activities are often neglected in our haste to perform more urgent jobs.

Using this distinction between different types of tasks, we can see that the greatest waste of time occurs when we are preoccupied by activities which are neither important nor urgent (see time-wasters, pp. 30–3). And the tasks which demand immediate action are those which are both urgent and important. In order to avoid unnecessary stress, try to arrange your daily timetable to maximise the time you spend in performing *important* rather than *urgent* jobs.

Review the time you spend on different subjects/courses

Allocating study time equally to all your subjects or courses is a major challenge for students. For one thing, you may be far more interested in one topic rather than another. Accordingly, you will tend to spend more time on it than on other topics. In addition, the unstructured nature of university life means that advice on time-management is difficult to obtain. But perhaps a simple adjustment to your daily routine may help. Specifically, you should develop the habit of spending ten minutes each night in reviewing what you did on each of your major subject areas during that day. Even if this review shows that you did nothing in a particular area, you have succeeded in alerting yourself to the danger of neglecting certain areas on your course.

Schedule different jobs for different times

It is a good idea to schedule different types of study tasks for different times of the day. Although students vary in their preferred learning times (some people are 'night owls' whereas others are 'larks'), research suggests that jobs which require intense concentration (e.g. revising for an exam or writing a term paper) should be undertaken during uninterrupted times early in the morning. The big advantage of doing your most demanding work at this time is captured by the maxim 'If you do it early, *it's done sooner*'. As the day progresses, lots of other jobs will clamour for your attention. Therefore, it is important to begin your studies as early as possible to avoid being gridlocked by having too many jobs to do at the one time. Using the traffic light analogy we referred to in the last chapter, you should interpret the early part of the morning as a green light signalling time to go for your work. Meanwhile, routine tasks which require less mental effort (such as borrowing books from the library) may be performed later in the day.

Make an effective timetable: Practical tips

How much study time do you have available each week? Make out a timetable for a typical week and assess *realistically* how many hours of private study time are available to you for a given week during term – taking into account other demands on your time which arise from such activities as working (if you have a part-time job), commuting to university, mealtimes, coffee breaks, exercise activities, hobbies and sports, social life, leisure periods, time to perform routine chores and, of course, sleep time. When you have established how many study hours are available to you, identify your specific study goals (see Chapter 2).

Write down your study tasks under three headings: short-term goals (i.e. daily or weekly – e.g. to read the chapter in a textbook which was referred to in a lecture today); intermediate-term goals (e.g. to conduct library research for an essay that has to be submitted by the end of this term or semester) and long-term goals (e.g. to perform as well as possible in my end-of-year examinations).

Always specify a starting time and a *finishing* time for your study session. Without a finishing time, your mind will begin to wander. Before you begin to study, write down 2–3 specific study questions (see Chapter 5). As the phrase goes, '*ink them*, don't just think them'. For each of these study goals, list 2–3 relevant actions that you can take which will bring you one step nearer to your goal – the more specific your action steps, the better. Next, specify a brief time-frame for each step (e.g. '10.00–10.50. Go to Library to obtain key references mentioned in class today').

Try to arrange your study time in blocks of 2–3 hours – devoting approximately 50 minutes to a different study question (see advice on summarising skills in Chapter 5). At the end of each 50-minute study period, you should take a 3–5 minute break. After you have finished a 2–3 hour block, spend 5–10 minutes reviewing what you have learned. Specifically, you should ask yourself what information you have acquired and how it relates to what you already know. Glance over your summary sheets (see Chapter 5) as you review your progress.

Try to make sure that the academic tasks which require the greatest mental work or concentration are scheduled for your best times each day (those periods when you feel most energetic and alert).

If your timetable is not helping you to achieve progress, arrange an appointment to meet your academic tutor (e.g. a staff member) and seek advice from him or her on how best to achieve your goal. When arranging to meet academic staff in your department or faculty, please note the person's official 'office hours' (during which lecturers/professors are available to meet students). If these times do not suit you, perhaps you could write a brief note to the relevant lecturer/professor to seek a formal appointment.

As I mentioned earlier, a good practical guideline is to allow at least two hours of private study for every formal lecture hour on your timetable. Additional time will have to be devoted to homework assignments such as practicals (e.g. drawing in Engineering).

The importance of regular exercise

To conclude, regular physical exercise (as gained, for example, through walking, cycling, swimming, aerobics, competitive sport or working out in a gym) is important both for bodily health and for mental well-being. Research suggests that physical exercise offers three potential benefits. First, it provides a welcome release or time out from the monotony of studying. Second, it refreshes your mind and increases your sense of vitality and alertness when you re-commence your work. In other words, it produces a positive rebound effect. Finally, physical exercise serves as a buffer against stress – increasing one's resistance to anxiety attacks, depression and many psychophysiological ailments (e.g. headaches). In view of these findings, you should allocate a certain amount of time every week for physical (but not necessarily competitive) exercise. A healthy body encourages a successful mind.

Summary

Without self-discipline, the free time that is available in university can easily become *wasted* time. This chapter provided some practical tips designed to increase the efficiency of your study time. I began by asking you to complete a time log of your study activities for a given day. Then I reviewed some problems which could serve as potential time-wasters for students. In particular, three obstacles to efficient study were analysed. These factors included not knowing how or where to start your work, engaging in procrastination, and indulging in task hopping (i.e. flitting from one activity to another depending on your prevailing mood). In an effort to combat these problems, I presented a range of practical time-management techniques. Included here was advice on daily goal-setting, establishing study priorities and routines, the need for brief but regular learning sessions, scheduling your academic tasks to coincide with periods of maximum alertness and on the distinction between urgent and important jobs. Tips on making effective timetables as well as on the benefits of regular exercise were also provided.

4. Listening and Taking Notes at the Same Time: Learning from Lectures

'Not all his class attend his lectures. Of those who attend, only half listen to what he says. Of those who attend and listen, only half understand. Of those who attend, and listen, and understand, only half remember. Of those who attend and listen and understand and remember, only half agree.' (Former President of Yale University, *UCD News*, April/May, 1986)

'A lecture is an experience in which one is privileged to hear a great mind in communion with itself' (attributed to Professor Denis Donohue, 1970–1971)

'A professor is one who talks in someone else's sleep' (attributed to W. H. Auden)

Introduction

Since the Middle Ages, the lecture has been the most popular teaching method in university education. Using this method, a lecturer typically delivers an audio-visual discourse on a chosen topic for about 50 minutes. During this period of time, attending students are encouraged to take relevant notes on the material presented. Therefore, the success of a lecture depends, at least in part, on efficient note-taking skills. But as you received little or no training in these skills at school, how can you be sure that you are benefiting fully from the lectures which you attend in university? For example, do you try to take down everything that your lecturers say in class? If so, is it hard to keep up with them? And if not, is it difficult to know which points to note and which ones to ignore? If such problems bother you, don't despair. Most students find it difficult to adjust to the lecturing system in university. The main reason for this problem is that note-taking is a *skill* which requires you to switch attention rapidly between listening and writing. And remember that people can speak faster than they write – so there is always likely to be a mismatch between lecturing and note-taking. Accordingly, just as you have developed certain reading habits (see p. 8), you have also acquired a preferred note-taking style. For example, you may act like a sponge in class, trying to mop up everything that the lecturer says.

Alternatively, you may see yourself as a prospector of ideas, sifting lecture content for nuggets of gold (Browne & Keeley, 1994). Either way, one thing is certain. Taking lecture notes effectively not only helps you to keep track of what was covered in class but also improves your ability to *think* about your subject while you are being taught. As Palmer & Pope (1984) proposed, good note-taking 'combines the recording of useful information with alert thinking' (p. 87). To illustrate, good note-takers have learned the art of thinking along with their lecturer to such an extent that they can anticipate what s/he is likely to say next. By contrast, poor note-takers are so preoccupied with taking down every word uttered in class that they sacrifice understanding for detail. In view of the importance of note-taking, this chapter will provide some practical tips on what to do before, during and after classes in order to enhance your understanding and memory of lecture material.

I shall proceed as follows. To begin with, I shall consider briefly the challenge of learning from lectures. As we shall see, this task requires you to develop the skill of thinking and writing simultaneously. Then I shall explore some common barriers to learning from lectures. Finally, I shall suggest some practical strategies which will help you to turn lecture attendance into an active learning experience rather than a meaningless obligation.

The challenge of learning from lectures

Lectures offer several advantages as instructional tools. To begin with, they provide an efficient way of transmitting information to large groups of people in a relatively short duration. In addition, their flexibility ensures that they can be used for an impressive range of educational purposes. For example, they can provide a frame of reference for a new topic, disseminate recent advances in an existing body of knowledge and/or encourage critical evaluation of a given theory or field. Third, the drama and immediacy of a well-crafted lecture can inspire audiences in emotional ways. Indeed, long after you have left university, you will still remember vividly those lecturers whose enthusiasm proved to be contagious. But each of these advantages assumes that you have *remembered* some aspect of the lecture. After all, you cannot be said to have learned something unless you have retained some memory of it. And this leads us to consider two disadvantages of lectures. First, if students attending a class adopt too passive a listening role, they may find it difficult to maintain their concentration. To illustrate, Peoples (1988) claims that a listener's attention wanders after only about *eight minutes* of a formal lecture! If this figure applies to you, then you need to learn ways of re-focusing rapidly during lectures in order to avoid wasting your time (see also Chapter 6). Compounding this problem is a second difficulty. To explain, university lecturers tend to be hired more for their *research* skills than for their ability to teach effectively. Therefore, although they may know a lot about their subject, they may not be skilful teachers. For example, they may believe that their task in presenting a lecture is to cram as much information into your minds as possible in the time allocated. Therefore, they may race along at breakneck speed – oblivious to the restlessness and frustration which they engender. Taken together, these disadvantages of lectures can pose problems for students. But these problems are not insurmountable. In fact, they can be overcome quite easily – once you understand what your main task is in attending a lecture. So what does this task actually involve?

Superficially, the task of listening to a lecture seems no different from participating in an everyday conversation. Specifically, you have to decode what someone says to you as they utter between 100 and 200 words per minute (Matlin, 1998). However, paying attention to a lecture differs significantly from other forms of listening. To begin with, it involves *taking notes* – not something which occurs in every-day conversational exchanges. Furthermore, whereas formal lectures tend to be monologues, conversations are interactive with participants alternating regularly between the roles of speaker and listener. Finally, good listeners use strategies (e.g. asking questions in their minds such as 'What conclusion is this leading to?') in order to *anticipate* what is likely to be said next. A more technical analysis of the psycho-logical processes involved in listening to a lecture is presented in Box 4.1. Having explored the challenge of listening to a lecture, let us now consider some myths concerning note-taking.

Barriers to learning from lectures

If you want to learn from lectures, you need to be able to alternate rapidly between listening and taking notes, while ignoring back-ground noise and other distractions in the lecture hall. Having explored some aspects of the listening process, I shall now consider the main barriers to effective learning in lectures.

Not preparing for the lecture

Do you engage in any form of preparation before attending lectures? Probably not – because most students believe that the only preparation required is to arrive with a pen and paper before the class begins. But

Box 4.1 *Decoding a lecture: What goes on in your mind?*

According to Smyth *et al.* (1994), decoding a lecture, in a crowded, noisy theatre with lots of distractions present, is a sophisticated cognitive activity which involves several mental processes working together in less than a few seconds. To begin with, your perceptual and word-recognition processes need to be working satisfactorily in order to segment the stream of speech sounds that emanate from the lecturer's mouth. Next, you need to be able to parse or analyse the syntactic structure of the sentences uttered by the lecturer. This task involves a great deal of prediction. For example, determiner words like 'a' or 'the' usually indicate the beginning of a noun phrase whereas words like 'because' suggest that a new clause is about to occur in a sentence. At this stage, your 'phonological loop' (the component of your working memory system that is responsible for maintaining speech sounds for about 1.5 seconds – your 'inner voice') is necessary because in order to understand a long sentence, you need to be able to store the first few words in your inner voice while you process the last few words. Next, in order to make any sense of what the lecturer is saying, you must be able to use your comprehensive store of relevant background knowledge to comprehend the sentences being uttered. Finally, you need to be able summarise the most important points of the lecture in a form that you will understand later when you review your notes.

if you fail to prepare for lectures, is it any wonder that your mind begins to wander during them? (see also Chapter 6). Perhaps the best way to prepare for a lecture is to spend 3–5 minutes glancing over any relevant lecture notes from previous weeks so that you are mentally attuned to what will be covered next.

Trying to write down every word the lecturer says

A common myth among university students is that they have to write down every single word uttered by a lecturer during class. This belief is false for several reasons. First, trying to record everything that a lecturer says at normal conversational speed is futile because people can *speak* faster than they can write. Second, the purpose of a lecture is to illuminate key points which you can explore further through private study rather than to provide the last word on the subject. Finally, good lecturers are skilled at making the same point in several different ways, thereby allowing you to take a breather during a class. In order to explore your note-taking style, see Box 4.2.

Box 4.2 *The importance of being a prospector*

Although people vary considerably in the way in which they like to receive information, research suggests that successful students act more like prospectors than sponges when taking notes in lectures (Browne & Keeley, 1994). Whereas weak students believe that they have to soak up every word uttered by the lecturer, successful counterparts pan the content for key ideas (nuggets) which they can summarise. Apparently, this prospector style of note-taking helps students to become active and critical listeners rather than passive transcribers of information.

Failing to impose a structure on what the lecturer says

Have you ever heard people talking to each other in a foreign language? If so, they seem to be speaking very fast and using a continuous stream of words. This experience is called the segmentation problem because it stems from not knowing how to impose *boundaries* on unfamiliar words. Of course, we have no trouble in recognising gaps between familiar words in our own language. But interestingly, these boundaries we perceive in familiar speech are imaginary. Thus acoustic signal analysis reveals that there are almost as many boundaries and pauses *within* the words we use as between them. It seems as though we use our knowledge of the meanings of words to impose an organisation on the continuous stream of speech sounds that we hear. Listening to lectures is a bit like trying to segment speech sounds: in order to understand them, you need to impose an *organisation* on what you hear. I shall explain how to do this in the next section.

When taking lecture notes, try to be a prospector not a sponge

Failing to identify what the lecturer emphasises as important

Most lecturers use verbal signposts to signal to their audiences that certain details of their presentation are especially important. For example, they may use such phrases as 'In summary . . . ' or 'The key point here is . . .' in order to convey the message 'Here is a crucial point that I would like you to note' . By listening carefully for such phrases, you will be able to identify a few key ideas in every lecture that you attend.

Losing your concentration

It is difficult, if not impossible, to concentrate fully on a lecture delivered for 50 minutes. Accordingly, as emphasised elsewhere in this book (see Chapters 1 and 5), you need to re-focus your concentration regularly by questioning yourself silently. Useful questions in this regard include 'What is the main point here?' or 'How does this information relate to what I already know?'

Practical ways of getting the most out of your lectures

In order to improve your note-taking skills, you need to become a more active learner. You can do this by developing the habit of performing certain tasks before, during and after lectures. Here is a summary of these learning tasks for lectures.

Develop a pre-lecture routine

Most top-class performers (e.g. actors, athletes, musicians) have developed characteristic sequences of thoughts and actions (called routines) to help them to prepare for important events. These routines are valuable because they encourage planning (i.e. focusing only on present actions that are under one's own control) rather than worrying (i.e. speculating about future events that lie outside one's control) (see Chapter 6). In general, less successful students have fewer and less consistent routines than successful ones. Given this finding, here are some suggested activities which may form part of your pre-lecture routine.

- Arrive 3–5 minutes before the lecture begins so that you can get a good seat (preferably close to where the lecturer will stand so that you can obtain a clear view of the board, screen or computer being used).

- Before the lecture begins, skim though your lecture notes to find out what was covered in the last class on this course. It helps if your notes for each course are stored in separate folders. Ring-binders are useful because they allow you to re-arrange your notes conveniently.

- Put the date and name of the lecture at the top of a your page.

- Make sure that you begin your notes for each lecture on a separate page. This will help you to file them properly later.

Establish a comfortable note-taking style: More is not necessarily better

The way in which you take lecture notes may reveal your approach to learning. In general, as I explained in Box 4.2 (p. 46), adopting a prospector role in note-taking seems to work well. But remember that your lecture notes are only a *means* to an end (namely, private study) – not an end in themselves. Unfortunately, many students fall into the trap of believing that just because they possess a set of lecture notes on a topic, they understand it fully. But possession is no guarantee of understanding. As Anthony Burgess (1966) once remarked, 'the possession of a book becomes a substitute for reading it'. Similarly, having a photocopy of something is no guarantee that you will understand it (a myth called 'the seduction of reproduction'; see also Chapter 5 and Chapter 9). So, don't waste much time in photocopying lecture notes. Their main function is to guide your private study. Accordingly, there is little point in re-writing them in order to make them look tidier. It is much better to have untidy but regularly reviewed lecture notes than to have tidy unread ones!

Organise the lecture in your mind

It is difficult to understand or remember information which lacks a structure. For example, if we can classify something we are told, then we can link the new information with what we already know. To demonstrate this principle for yourself, try the exercise in Box 4.3.

The purpose of this exercise is to show you that we can improve our note-taking skills by trying to *categorise* or impose some meaning on anything which we wish to remember (see also Chapter 8).

Ask questions in your mind
Just before the lecturer starts, try to think up a few questions which might be covered by the presentation. As I shall explain in Chapter 8, questioning facilitates depth of processing of the material to be covered.

Divide and conquer
To improve their note-taking skills, some students find it helpful to divide lectures into three parts: the beginning (introduction); the middle (central theme and supporting details); and the end (conclusions). In the introduction, the lecturer usually reminds you of what s/he covered in the last class and gives a brief overview of the theme of the current lecture. Then s/he outlines details of the main evidence or arguments. Finally, the last part of a lecture is usually devoted to a review of the conclusions which arise from the evidence presented. So the idea is to listen very carefully at the beginning and the end, and to be selective about the notes that you take during the middle section of the lecture as this information can be obtained in the recommended readings.

In the first few minutes of any class, the lecturer tends to 'set the scene' for the talk using such strategies as asking you rhetorical

---

Box 4.3 *Exploring the importance of organisation*

A key skill required to take effective notes from lectures is the ability to organise them using appropriate schemas or headings. To illustrate, imagine a lecturer providing the following details during his/her presentation. Would you be able to make any sense of them as they appear below?

The procedure is really quite simple. First you have to arrange items into different groups. Sometimes, one pile may be sufficient – but it depends on how much material has accumulated since the last operation. If you can't do the job yourself, then you may have to bring the stuff elsewhere. Otherwise, you're ready to go. But try not to not to do too much at the one time. A mistake at this stage could ruin one of your favourite items. Although this task may seem quite complicated at the beginning, you will soon accept it as a weekly routine. And while the job is in progress, you can do other things with your time. After it is finished, however, you will have to re-arrange the items into piles and take them to the next stage of the cycle. Eventually, they will be used again and the whole process will have to be repeated (based on Bransford & Johnson, 1972).

Most students find the passage above incomprehensible. This is so because the text lacks a clear frame of reference – something to help you to organise it properly. But if you knew in advance the *heading* used to describe this passage (try to guess it before turning to the back of the chapter), you would find it a lot easier to memorise. When you have learned the appropriate schema for this passage, re-read the text and notice how quickly all of the words make sense to you. This happens because the heading activates prior knowledge which you already have about the topic (see also Chapter 8). The practical implication of this finding is that it shows the importance of asking questions like 'What part of the course does this apply to?'. The answer to the exercise above is given on p. 55.

---

questions, giving you a brief overview of what s/he intends to cover or by trying to link what is about to be discussed with what was covered in the previous lecture. These opening remarks are vital to your learning because they establish 'advance organisers' which will increase your understanding of, and memory for, what is about to be discussed. Unfortunately, many students miss out on these key points because they arrive late, look around for where their friends are sitting or make noise by shuffling their bags or notes. These distractions prevent you from being properly 'tuned in' to the class. Indeed, a failure to pay attention to the initial few moments of a presentation may explain why students lose their concentration so easily during class. So pay attention to the early part of a message because understanding the specific theme or purpose of the lecture is half the battle – you can look up the precise details or supporting evidence after class in the prescribed textbook for the course.

The main part of a lecture is usually devoted to an explanation of details – such as historical issues, theories, principles or research findings. Because of the amount of material covered, it may be difficult to make notes on everything that is presented to you. But try to make sure that you write down key names and dates, ideas or headings, especially if the lecturer gives some reason as to why these details are particularly important.

The last few minutes of a lecture are vital because they usually contain the lecturer's summary of relevant conclusions. Unfortunately, many students miss these points for two main reasons. Firstly, the lecturer may have closed his or her notes or switched off the projector – thereby conveying the false impression that the talk is over. Secondly, the student may be preparing for his or her next class and may have packed for a quick getaway.

Overall, therefore, you should be aware of the 'primacy recency' principle when taking notes from lectures. This principle shows that people tend to remember best what happens at the beginning and at the end of a message – but they miss out on many of the details in the middle of the class.

Look out for trigger words

As I explained earlier, effective listening is an *active* process in which one person tries to make sense of, and anticipate, what the other is saying. Using some active listening principles, you could benefit from the following advice.

- Spot any signpost words and/or transition phrases ('The main point of this is . . .' or 'What this really means is that . . .' or 'So, the principle here is . . .') used by the lecturer

- Pay attention to the points or statements which a lecturer repeats frequently or explains in different ways during the lecture

- Try to think along with the lecturer by predicting what's likely to be said next

- Make sure to note any examples used by the lecturer and try to be sure you understand the point which they illustrate. If not, ask your lecturer about the significance of the example as soon as possible

- Ask yourself how this new information relates to what you already know

- Get the name of at least one reference for further reading. Where can I learn more about this topic?

Use abbreviations

Because lecturers tend to deliver their material at normal speaking speed, you will have to learn to use abbreviations when taking notes (e.g. 'expt' for 'experiment' or 'FR' for 'French Revolution'). This is a good idea – but please make sure that your shorthand is consistent. Otherwise, a variation in how you abbreviate a concept or term may lead to confusion when you try to decipher your notes.

- Usually, in the first few sentences, the lecturer will set the scene for the presentation, providing a brief summary of what was covered last day or giving an overview of what s/he intends to cover in the lecture. Try to summarise this information briefly.

- Make sure to write down any references that the lecturer mentions during the class. You can check these references later in the library. If you did not hear them properly, go along to the lecturer after the class (or during stated office hours) and ask him or her for relevant details.

Review your notes after the lecture

Many students take good lecture notes – but fail to use them adequately afterwards. In this section, I shall consider how best to review and consult your lecture notes. Although students vary widely in how well they use their notes, one point is quite clear. The longer the delay between taking and reviewing your notes, the less benefit you will derive from them. So it is best to skim through your lecture notes on the same day as you record them. Let us consider now the basis for, and implications of, this idea.

Just as we learned that studying is enriched by engaging in a brief review period (see the principle of overlearning, p. 105), it should come as no surprise to you that what you learn from lectures will be enhanced by performing certain tasks on your notes. Three tasks are particularly important in this regard. First, you should try to make a connection between the notes from your last lecture and those from earlier lectures on the course. Ask yourself such questions as: 'Why were the lectures presented in that particular sequence?' or 'Can I detect any obvious pattern across the lectures on the course?' or 'What are the most important ideas that receive regular emphasis in this course?' Next, you should try to construct 2–3 topic sentences for the lecture. The idea here is to construct a short paragraph which condenses the main points of the lecture and helps you to consider how it relates to what you already know about the topic in question. Third, you should go to the library to look up the key names or specific references cited by your lecturer. It is helpful to allocate the same time for this activity every week.

Before concluding this chapter, let us discuss an issue which many students regard as the solution to the problem of missing something said in class. Is it a good idea to tape lectures? As Box 4.4 indicates, tape-recording lectures is unwise. Apart from the ethical problems which are raised by recording people's speech without their permission, taping is too passive and uncritical to promote effective learning.

Summary

Your success in learning from lectures in university will depend significantly upon your note-taking skills. Specifically, unless you can alternate rapidly between the tasks of thinking and writing, while simultaneously listening to the lecturer and filtering out distractions, you will be lost in the classroom. Unfortunately, few students receive any advice or training in school on how to cope with situations where the teacher speaks faster than one can write. Accordingly, they make the mistake of trying to take down every word uttered by the lecturer rather than panning for gold – or listening selectively for the main ideas presented. In view of this problem, the purpose of this chapter was to provide some practical tips on what to do before, during and after class in order to enhance your ability to understand and remember the key points of any lecture. I began by exploring the challenge of listening to a lecture. Briefly, this task involves thinking along with the lecturer so that you can understand and record the main ideas or information which s/he presents. But several obstacles can hamper this activity. For example, failing to prepare for, or impose an organisational structure on, lectures makes note-taking hazardous. In addition, not knowing how to spot signpost words (verbal cues to important ideas) makes it difficult to distinguish between key ideas and trivial information in a lecture. Therefore, I provided some

Box 4.4 *To tape or not to tape? Is it helpful to record lectures?*

Given the importance of taking notes accurately, is it a good idea to use a tape recorder in class? At first glance, the mechanical recording of lectures seems like a great idea. After all, it seems to provide a simple and convenient method of capturing every word of the lecture. Unfortunately, closer inspection of this practice shows that tape recording of lectures has several serious drawbacks. First, it is ethically questionable (and may contravene university regulations) if it is conducted without the explicit permission of the lecturer. Also, it may be necessary to obtain permission from your class-mates – especially if they ask questions or contribute to a class discussion during the lecture. Lecturers usually dislike speaking into tape recorders simply because the spontaneity of a presentation is hampered by the knowledge that every remark will be recorded. In a similar vein, lecturers are concerned about the prospect of tapes being copied and transcripts of their notes being passed on to other students. But apart from these objections, there are two major psychological reasons why tape recording of lectures is inadvisable for students. One difficulty is that recording lectures may induce complacency in students. Thus the act of taking notes while listening to a lecture forces you to take an active role in thinking critically about the content of a lecture. Conversely, having a tape recorder encourages a passive mode of learning in which the mind is free to wander due to the false assumption that the information that is going into the recorder now will go into your mind later. Another problem is that you may be very disappointed with the quality of the tape recording that you make in lectures. You will probably find a lot more noise on the tape (coughs, seats shifting, talking among students) than you noticed at the time you were listening to the lecturer. This occurs because the mind, unlike any mechanical device that has been invented yet, can filter out distractions at the same time as they occur. In summary, taping lectures is unethical and unwise, unless there is a very good reason (e.g. a visual disability) which precludes you from taking notes in the normal manner.

practical tips on getting the most out of lectures. Included here were such strategies as developing a brief pre-class routine (where you flick over what was covered in the preceding lecture in the series) and trying to organise the lecture into a beginning, middle and end. I also explored the value of asking questions in your mind before the lecture begins, paying attention to signpost words and phrases, and trying to condense the central ideas of the lecture once it is over. Finally, I explained why tape recording lectures is less effective than is taking notes from them manually.

Answer to exercise in Box 4.3 (p. 50)

The passage of text was about washing clothes.

5. Improving Your Reading and Summarising Skills: Tackling Textbooks

'Curiously enough, one cannot read a book: one can only re-read it. A good reader, a major reader, an active and creative reader is a re-reader'
(Vladimir Nabokov, 1980)

Introduction

One of the greatest differences between university and school concerns the nature and amount of background reading which students have to conduct for their courses. Whereas the total number of textbooks prescribed for most school examinations barely reaches double figures, the reading list for a *single* course in university may be several pages long! Compounding this quantitative challenge is a qualitative factor – the fact that you are also expected to *think critically* about what you read in university. In other words, you not only have to read more in university, but also to read differently from the way in which you read things in school (see the above quote from Nabokov). But has anyone ever taught you *how* to extract maximum information from what you read? If not, then you may benefit from some practical advice in this area. Therefore, the purpose of this chapter is to show you how to *think* while you read.

I shall begin with a brief explanation of what reading involves. Then, I shall provide some practical advice on coping with reading lists. Next, following analysis of some learning strategies used by expert readers, I shall show you how to use a reading technique called the 'PQRR' method. This technique trains you to process written material deeply and efficiently. Then, I shall consider the hazards of passive methods of learning from textbooks. These methods include underlining, transcription and photocopying. Next, I shall explain how to improve your summarising skills. Finally, I shall show you that when you know what to look for, you *can* sometimes judge a book by its cover!

Reading

We take our ability to read so much for granted that we become aware of it only when it *fails* in some way. For example, when we stumble over an unfamiliar technical term (e.g. what does 'homoscedasticity' mean?) or stare blankly at a foreign phrase (e.g. *inter alia)*, we suddenly discover that our word recognition skills have let us down. At such moments, we realise that reading is more complex than it seems. In fact it involves drawing conclusions from the text as well as processing the letters on the page. To test this idea for yourself, try the exercise in Box 5.1 overleaf.

Effective reading requires at least three types of information processing (Gagné, Yekovich & Yekovich, 1993). First, as Box 5.1 shows, you need to have access to relevant background knowledge. Next, your word recognition skills must be effortless or else your reading will be slow and cumbersome. Third, your ability to understand and remember what you read depends on such skills as asking specific questions before you begin and monitoring your comprehension regularly (also Chapter 1). Overall, therefore, reading is not a passive activity. Instead, it is best regarded as an active guessing game in which the reader converses with, or interrogates, the text. Paradoxically, readers do not absorb information passively from a passage of information. They *add* relevant background knowledge in order to decode it.

To illustrate the *constructive* nature of your reading, you should find that you have no difficulty in understanding the following sentence even though more than a third of the letters are missing.

Thx pxssxblx mexnxxg ox a sxxtenxe ix quxte exsy tx extxblxsh whxn yxur mxnd fillx ix thx gapx

If you cannot decipher this piece of text, please turn to the summary at the end of the chapter for the answer. But if you have worked out what the sentence means, then you have shown that reading is a *constructive* process because it involves the imaginative 'building up' of meaning. Ironically, it is this constructive process, or the automatic habit of filling in the blanks, which explains why it can be difficult for us to spot typing errors when we we proof-read our own writing. For example, did you notice that the word 'we' occurred twice in the previous sentence?

Fluent reading requires mastery of a number of cognitive tasks (Pressley & McCormick, 1995). First, we need to move our eyes swiftly across the page in order to encode (or take in) the text visually. Second, to facilitate comprehension, we need rapid access

> Box 5.1   Reading and drawing conclusions
>
> When we read things, we automatically draw conclusions from the words which we see. Consider the following two sentences. Do they make sense as they are presented, or do you have to use some background knowledge to interpret them?
>
> Sentence 1   *When the attacker went down in the box, the referee blew the whistle and pointed to the spot*
>
> Sentence 2   *When the policewoman held up her hand, the man stopped and rolled down his window*
>
> Passage 3   *Mary heard the ice-cream van coming down the road. She ran into her house to get some money*
>
> Most readers conclude that sentence 1 referred to a penalty awarded during a football or a hockey match. But notice that the word penalty is not mentioned in the sentence – it's something which you inferred from the text using your background knowledge of sporting terminology. Similarly, in order to interpret sentence 2, you need to assume that the man was driving a car and that police officers have the power to request drivers to stop. Finally, in passage 3, people tend to integrate the two sentences in a causal manner. For example, they conclude that Mary went into her house in order to obtain some money to buy ice-cream. But notice that this was never actually stated in the text – the reader supplies the missing details by going beyond the information provided. Taken together, these passages show you that reading is not simply a matter of processing letters. It also requires the unconscious use of relevant background knowledge *to build an understanding* of what was intended.

to a large vocabulary of word meanings (our mental lexicon). Interestingly, it has been estimated that typical university students can understand over 100,000 word meanings in their native language. Third, our short-term (or working) memory must be able to retain the initial words of a sentence while the latter part is being processed. Finally, readers must be able to use relevant background knowledge to decipher words and to fill in the gaps when necessary.

Do these principles help us to distinguish expert readers from novices? Wyatt *et al.* (1993) attempted to answer this question recently. Briefly, they began by asking 15 accomplished university professors to select an interesting journal article that was in their field of expertise. These professors were then requested to think aloud as they read the selected articles. Their comments were recorded on audiotape and their eye-movements were also assessed. The results revealed a consistent pattern of reading behaviour among these expert researchers. In particular, they

- looked for information relevant to their own research goals
- summarised key points frequently
- tried to anticipate information in the text
- searched forwards and backwards for specific information
- re-read sentences which were unclear
- evaluated new information from the text in the light of what they already knew
- checked their progress as they read through the article

Does this pattern of expert reading behaviour remind you of anything you encountered earlier in this book? If not, turn back to Box 1.2 in Chapter 1 (p. 8), where I explained some reading skills which distinguish successful from unsuccessful students.

In summary, expert readers are distinguished from novices in their use of active learning techniques. Specifically, they interrogate the text in search of answers to specific questions and check their understanding regularly. In short, they adopt a *conversational* approach to reading. Fortunately, you can copy this approach using the PQRR reading technique which I shall explain shortly. But before doing so, I would like to address the problem of coping with lengthy reading lists.

Coping with reading lists

A reading list is a compilation of the references (i.e. books and articles) which a lecturer deems to be relevant to a particular topic or course. Ideally, this list should encourage the student to go to the library or the bookshop in search of specific references. Unfortunately, all too often, reading lists are lengthy and forbidding – thereby demoralising, rather than inspiring, students. So how can you manage your reading lists effectively? Box 5.2 contains some practical tips for this task.

Box 5.2 *Managing your reading lists*

1. Photocopy your reading lists so that you can attach them to your notes as well as having copies elsewhere.

2. You do not have to read every item on the list. But you should try to distinguish between essential and recommended references. If this information is not stated explicitly, then you should ask the relevant lecturer for help on this issue.

3. Distinguish between primary and secondary sources. The former comprise original works whereas the latter contain commentaries on, or analysis of, this material. Although you may get away with reading only secondary sources, your under-standing of the material will be enhanced if you have read at least some of the original works (especially in Arts /Humanities subjects).

4. Write down the precise library location for each important reference on the reading list.

Assuming that you have decided which books you wish to tackle, the next step is to learn to read them thoroughly. And this brings us to an expert reading strategy called the PQRR technique.

Becoming an expert reader: The PQRR technique

One of the great pioneers of reading strategies was a researcher named Francis Robinson of Ohio State University. He devised the technique on which the PQRR strategy is based (Robinson, 1961). Briefly, the acronym PQRR stands for four key mental skills under-lying efficient reading. These skills are **p**reviewing, **q**uestioning, **r**eading and **r**eviewing. To illustrate these skills, imagine that you wish to read a specific chapter from a textbook on your course.

Preview – 'P'

To begin with, you should preview or survey the chapter briefly (for 2–3 minutes) before you read it in any detail. Failing to do this is like walking into a darkened room without first turning on the light (Deem, 1993). So, a preview will light up the material and will prevent you from getting lost in it. As you skim through the pages, try to get a picture of how the chapter is organised. Pay attention to the titles of the paragraphs and glance over any summaries that might be provided.

Previewing what you read is helpful in at least three ways. First, like the trailer of a film at a cinema, a preview gives you a taste of what is to come. Second, a quick survey of a chapter activates any relevant background knowledge which you might possess about the content. Third, previewing material helps to establish hooks or cues which facilitate later retrieval (see also Chapter 8).

Practical tips on previewing
- Look at the headings of the sections and paragraphs of the chapter in order to 'get a feel' for the way in which it is organised.

- Scan any pictures, charts, diagrams, graphs and tables.

- Look for signpost words which suggest important conclusions ('To summarise . . .' or 'Overall, . . .').

- Skim through any summaries which may be available at the end of the chapter.

Question – 'Q'

In Chapter 1, I explained that questioning is the key to active learning. To paraphrase Barrass (1982), questions can provide mental tin-openers which unlock even the most arcane academic theories. Therefore, just as I explained in Chapter 1, before reading your textbook, you should write down on a blank sheet of paper 2–3 specific questions which you wish to answer from the chapter. Examples of different types of questions for different subjects are contained in Box 5.3. Your study questions can come from a wide variety of sources. For example, your own interests (e.g. 'What caused the famine in Ireland?') or personal experience (e.g. 'How does advertising affect our buying behaviour?') may generate questions which you wish to explore. Similarly, a remark or question from one of your lecturers ('Do you think that computers will ever be regarded as intelligent?') could stimulate your interest. But if you're more practically

Box 5.3   *Sample study questions*

Subject	Topic	Question
Veterinary Medicine	Animal Science	What factors affect growth rate in animals?
Law	Constitutional Law	How does the Constitution regulate the Government's entry into, and departure from, office?
Science	Geology	How may silicate minerals be classified according to their atomic structure?
Medicine	Histology	What are the characteristic features of a monosynaptic reflex arc?
Statistics	Correlation	What is a correlation coefficient and how is it calculated?
Social Science	Social Policy	What factors led to the development of a Welfare State in Britain after World War II?
Physiotherapy/ Radiography	Biochemistry	Why are some amino acids referred to as non-essential?
Engineering	Manufacturing Technology	What is re-crystallisation?
Agricultural Science	Chemistry	Why does sodium form an anion but magnesium does not?
Italian	Grammar	What are the basic rules for the use of definite and indefinite articles in Italian?
History	Modern Irish History	What caused the Great Famine of the 1840s?
Marketing	Advertising	What constitutes 'good' advertising?
Accountancy	Fixed Assets	What are 'fixed assets' and how can we value them?
Science	Biology	How does a cell synthesise a protein molecule from an mRNA template?

minded, then perhaps you might be motivated best by a question which appeared on a previous year's examination paper ('How are molecular techniques used in the attempt to diagnose diseases?'). Regardless of their source, questions facilitate active learning. Remember – successful students have questions in search of answers whereas unsuccessful students have answers in search of questions.

Practical tips on questioning

• What is the main theme, idea or learning point in this chapter?

• What evidence, arguments or examples are cited in support of this central theme?

• How does this theme relate to what I already know?

Read – 'R'

Read the chapter carefully with your study questions in mind. This conversational style of reading is what experts use to enable them to *think* while they read. As you make your way through the chapter, make brief notes as outline answers to your study questions. Material is relevant if it provides answers to your specific study questions but irrelevant if it fails to do so.

Practical tips on reading

• Always read with a pen and paper beside you. Remember that you're *looking for answers* to 2–3 specific questions

• Write down any information which seems to provide answers to any of your study questions

• Try to locate a 'topic sentence' which summarises what the author believes to be the most important point in a paragraph or chapter

• Slow down if you come to a difficult passage. If necessary, you should go back ('I can't understand this point: I'd better go back a few paragraphs') or forwards ('I'll skip ahead to see if this point is clarified in a later section') if you do not understand something

• Note any difficult technical terms so that you can look them up later

Review – 'R'

The final stage of active reading consists of checking your understanding of the material by *reviewing* what you have learned. One way of doing this is by examining the notes on your summary sheet and checking the degree to which they answer your initial study questions. Alternatively, if you participate in a regular study group with some class-mates, you could explain what you learned from the chapter and encourage your listeners to ask you questions about this material. When you have finished reviewing what you have learned, you should then consult another textbook with the same set of study questions in mind. Comparing answers from different textbooks to the same study questions encourages critical thinking (see also Chapter 7).

Practical tips on reviewing

- Pause from time to time to ask yourself what you learned from the chapter

- Glance over your summary sheets (i.e. the answers to your study questions) before you put away your books

Now that you have discovered the value of the PQRR reading technique, it is important to compare active and passive ways of learning from textbooks.

Box 5.4 *Using the PQRR technique*

Choose a chapter from a textbook which you wish to study. Then, using the PQRR approach, fill in the details below (based on Deem, 1993).

Step 1 Preview the chapter
Skim through the pages of this chapter for 3–5 minutes using the practical tips outlined earlier on previewing skills. Then see if you can answer the following questions

- What topic does the chapter cover? Can you turn this topic into a question?

- What 'trigger words' or ideas (if any!) come to mind (e.g. names of theorists) when you think about this topic? Any snippets of knowledge should be noted below.

Step 2 Formulate 2–3 specific questions
What are your specific study questions for this chapter?

_____

_____

_____

Step 3 Read with your questions in mind
Read through the text with your 2–3 study questions in mind. Pause from time to time to check your progress by asking yourself: what have I learned so far? Summarise relevant information (e.g. definitions, theories) on a sheet of paper beside each of your questions but ignore all other details.

Step 4 Review your summary sheet
When you have finished reading the chapter, ask yourself:

* What did I learn?

_____

_____

* How does it relate to what I already know?

_____

_____

Learning from books: The hazards of underlining, transcribing and photocopying

Unless they have been trained to use the PQRR approach, most students think that the best way to learn from a textbook is simply to read it from cover to cover, *highlighting* the most important points as they go along. Alternatively, they may spend hours *transcribing* textbook material into their notes. A third popular learning strategy involves *photocopying* as much of the book as possible. Unfortunately, each of these three approaches suffers from serious weaknesses.

To begin with, consider the practice of highlighting (with 'dayglo' markers) or underlining selected passages of text (using a pen or pencil). Clearly, the assumption here is that when such passages are re-read, the salient parts of the text will stand out conspicuously.

Unfortunately, underlining is an ineffective learning technique for several reasons. First, it does not take account of 'habituation' effects whereby people stop paying attention to something distinctive because they get used to it over time (which explains, for example, why we may only notice a mechanical clock when it *stops* ticking). More seriously, what you consider to be important in a given book depends significantly on what you *already* know about its content. And as your knowledge grows, so also does the likelihood that you will underline different passages from the book when you re-read it. Therefore, the more material you underline or highlight, the less it will capture your attention. Finally, underlining only marks the *textbook* – it will not create notes for you.

How effective is transcription as a learning strategy? The problem here is similar to that of trying to take down every word that a lecturer utters in class: the material goes straight into your notes, bypassing your mind. In other words, it does not lead to any form of elaboration or understanding on the part of the learner.

A third approach to learning from textbooks involves photo-copying everything in sight. In this case, students make the false

Textbooks are meant to be interrogated – not photocopied or underlined!

assumption that possession is equivalent to comprehension (a myth called the 'seduction of reproduction') – if you have a photocopy of an article, then you'll get around to understanding it some day. Of course, this theory is wrong. When Francis Bacon said that knowledge was power, he was *not* referring to stacks of un-read photocopies! Unless you can *paraphrase* accurately what is in a photocopied document, you may as well not have it at all.

Overall, the main weakness of such strategies as underlining/highlighting, transcription and photocopying is that they do not encourage the learner to produce a *summary* of the material being read. Accordingly, these techniques are mindless because they neither reduce the amount of material to be processed nor do they help the reader to distinguish between relevant and irrelevant information in the book. By contrast, the act of *summarising* a passage of text in *your own words* helps you develop a personal understanding of it (see also Chapter 8). Therefore, the best way to approach a textbook is to summarise the main ideas using an *active* learning technique such as the PQRR method rather engaging in transcription or photocopying.

Summarising and learning

The ability to make concise summaries of what you read has a number of theoretical and practical benefits. To begin with, summaries reduce the amount of material that you have to learn. Second, summarising compels you to *think critically* about what you are reading. Specifically, it forces you to distinguish between information which answers your study questions (relevant material) and that which has no bearing on them (irrelevant material). Third, producing a summary helps you to link the new material to what you already know – a process called elaborative rehearsal (see also Chapter 8). Finally, summary sheets provide skeletal answers which can be used in examinations.

Not surprisingly, our ability to summarise what we read improves with age and practice. Brown & Day (1983) found some significant differences between the summarising strategies used by children and those of university students. In particular, whereas the younger children (around six or seven years of age) were largely concerned with abbreviating the text, university students tried to *understand* it better by making a synopsis of the material in their own words.

Some tips on summarising material are given in Box 5.5 overleaf.

Box 5.5	Common summarising principles
Deletion	*Delete any information in your notes that is irrelevant to your study questions*
Topic sentence	*Look for, or invent, a topic sentence which describes the key points in the passage under scrutiny*
Integration	*Try to combine key phrases or information from different paragraphs into a single sentence*

Having provided some practical tips designed to improve your reading and summarising skills, I would like to conclude this chapter by offering some advice on judging a book by its cover.

Can you judge a book by its cover?

How does the design of an academic book affect its readability? Put differently, can you really judge the quality of a book by its cover?

Before I address these questions, here is a puzzle for you. Think of one of the main textbooks on your course. What are the names of the sections in this book which appear before the beginning of Chapter 1? If you have trouble in remembering sections such as the 'Preface', 'Foreword', 'Introduction' or 'Table of Contents', then you may not be paying enough attention to the *structure* of your books. Remember that the design of an academic textbook is not accidental. Each section (ranging from the title page to the subject or author index) offers clues to the organisation and layout of the content. By knowing this role, you can increase the efficiency of your learning from these books. Based on this principle, and borrowing some ideas from Marshall & Rowland (1993), here are some practical tips which will help you to judge a textbook by its cover.

Title and sub-title

Note the key words used (e.g. 'Human Memory') and look for any specific information revealed by sub-titles (e.g. 'A Connectionist Approach'). This sub-title will convey any theoretical perspectives favoured by the author.

Cover or dust-jacket

Skim through the information about the author and the book that may appear on the cover or dust-jacket. This information may provide a synopsis of the content of the book. It may also indicate any novel features of this book (e.g. its role in filling a gap in the literature or in providing a critical review of the field).

Biographical details of author(s)

Scan any biographical information on the author(s) of the book. Is s/he familiar to you? What are his or her qualifications or research interests? How does this book relate to any other books which s/he may have written in this field?

Publication details

You should be able to find out when a book was published, who published it and what edition it represents by looking at the reverse of the first or second page of it. This information is important because, in general, recent revisions of a book tend to contain more up-to-date research findings than do earlier editions of the same book.

Table of Contents

Flicking through the table of contents, you can establish quickly which of the chapters are most relevant to your personal needs. But if you are searching for a reference to a designated author's work, or for an explanation of a specific concept, then you should look up the author and subject index, respectively.

Preface / Foreword / Introduction

According to Deem (1993), reading the preface of a book is the next best thing to having a conversation with its author! The preface/ foreword/introduction usually provide answers to such questions as: Why was this book written? What makes it different from other books in the field? Is there anything new or different about the approach adopted by the author?

Chapter structure

As with the title of the book, the heading of each chapter indicates the topic which will receive coverage. And as I indicated on p. 8, a good way to increase your interest in it is simply to turn all titles into questions (e.g. 'Quadratic equations' becomes 'What are quadratic equations?'). In addition, the structure of the chapters is important. For example, is a summary provided at the end of each chapter? If so, you should read it before working your way through the chapter.

Glossary

If the book has a glossary at the end, skim through it in advance to see if you can recognise any of the terms it contains.

Bibliography and references

Is there a bibliography or list of references at the end of the book? If not, and if you cannot find any footnotes or end-notes either, then you should be sceptical of the academic credibility of the book. Without references, how can you validate the author's opinions? If you know some of the names of key researchers in this field, try to find out if these people are listed among the references.

Subject and author index

The index of a book will help you to check whether or not key names and concepts are referred to in the main body of the book. A short index may suggest that the book is not very comprehensive in scope.

Summary

One of the greatest challenges facing university students is to change their reading habits in order to keep up with the amount of background work which is required by all academic courses. Not surprisingly, research suggests that successful students tend to read more efficiently (they can extract more information in shorter time) than do their less successful counterparts. But what information processing techniques account for such efficiency and can they be incorporated into a useful reading strategy? The purpose of this chapter was to provide some practical answers to these vital questions. I began by explaining that reading entails far more than processing printed letters on a page. Instead, it is a constructive process in which we build up an understanding of the text by using background knowledge to draw conclusions about what is written. Accordingly, effective reading is an active guessing game in which the reader searches for clues in order to predict what will happen next. And that explains why expert readers not only interrogate the text in search of answers to their questions but also check their own progress in understanding this material as often as possible. Having explored some strategies used by expert readers, I then provided practical advice on how to cope with lengthy reading lists in university. In the next section, I explained the PQRR approach to expert reading – a strategy which involves four specific skills: **p**reviewing, **q**uestioning, **r**eading and **r**eviewing. This technique is extremely valuable in university as it trains you to process written material both deeply and efficiently. Then I warned of the hazards of passive methods of learning from textbooks. These methods included underlining, transcription and photocopying. The problem with these popular techniques is that they do not encourage you to summarise and think about what you are reading. In the next section, I explained the importance of condensing what you read and provided some practical tips on summarising skills. Finally, I suggested that sometimes, you *can* judge a book by its cover – or more precisely, by its layout and design.

Answer to demonstration (on p. 57)

'The possible meaning of a sentence is quite easy to establish when your mind fills in the gaps'.

6. Improving Your Concentration Skills

'Il was in my own little world, focusing on every shot. I wasn't thinking what score I was on or anything' (World Matchplay champion golfer, Darren Clarke, cited in Otway, 1999, p. 13)

Introduction

Imagine the concentration skill required to shoot a round of 60 in a major golf tournament. That is exactly what the Irish golfer Darren Clarke achieved at the 1999 European Open Championship. By contrast, have you ever discovered that you've been reading the same sentence in a textbook over and over again, without any comprehension, because your mind was miles away? Or do you often find yourself thinking of something else while listening to a lecture? If you can identify with either of these common experiences, then you know at first hand what losing your concentration means. And you're not alone with this problem. In a recent survey of over 1100 first-year university students, 27 per cent expressed concern about concentration problems which were afflicting their studies (Moran *et al.*, 1991). But take heart: if there is one thing worse than losing your concentration, it's *not knowing* that it's gone. Imagine staring at the same page for hours on end – literally lost in thought! Fortunately, such absent-mindedness is rare. But what exactly is concentration anyway? And why do our minds tend to wander so easily during study? What practical concentration strategies can we use to develop qualities like the tunnel vision that helped Darren Clarke to achieve his record-breaking score in golf. The purpose of this chapter is to provide some answers to these three questions.

To begin with, I shall explain what concentration involves. Next I shall explore what distractions are, where they come from and how to cope with them. Finally, I shall provide some practical techniques for improving your concentration skills. These methods include learning strategies described in earlier chapters (e.g. goal-setting and re-structuring; see Chapter 2) as well as some new techniques (e.g. visualisation). This section will also contain some advice on how to turn sources of pressure into enjoyable challenges.

What is concentration?

The term concentration refers to the ability to focus on what is most important in any situation while ignoring distractions. Trying to study for an examination while someone else is watching television in the same room requires this kind of selective attention. But there is more to concentration than simply blocking out potential distractors. For example, the way in which you *interpret* the task at hand affects your ability to focus on it. Consider the effect of background music on study skills (see also Box 2.3 in Chapter 2, p. 25). Briefly, research shows that students can concentrate quite effectively as long as they believe that they have the power to change the volume of the music in the background. But they tend to become quite agitated if *someone else* takes control of this music. Therefore, it is a loss of perceived control rather than a certain volume of background noise which tends to upset people most when studying. The implication of this finding is clear. The more control you believe that you can exert over any situation, the less it will distract you. Put differently, although you may not be able to change a distracting situation, you can *always* change how you react to it.

A useful way to understand concentration is to picture it as a *mental spotlight* which we shine at things which interest us. For example, as I explained in Chapter 5, you need to have a specific study question in mind before tackling a textbook. Accordingly, when studying, your mental spotlight must switch between this question and possible answers to it which emerge from your book. Anything else which attracts your attention (e.g. a displacement activity like tidying your room or having a cup of coffee – see p. 14) is a distraction. Therefore, the main principle of concentration is that as soon as you shine your mental spotlight on factors which are either outside your control or which are irrelevant to the task you wish to perform, then your mind will begin to drift. Put differently, in order to concentrate properly, make sure that what you think about is *specific*, *relevant* and *under your control*. Instead of vaguely promising yourself to 'do some reading' later, you could say: 'Between 7 p.m. and 8 p.m., I'm going to study my chemistry books in order to find out why sodium forms an anion whereas magnesium does not'.

In general, effective concentration involves at least three skills. First, you must have a clear objective in mind (e.g. a study question; see pp. 61–3). Second, you have to break up that objective into action-steps (i.e. tasks which take you a step nearer to your goal – see p. 21). Finally, you must remind yourself to re-focus periodically on those action steps or else you will think too far ahead. To illustrate these skills in action, consider the world of sport. When Jack Nicklaus, the famous golfer, was asked how he had managed to sink a 'pressure putt' in a close match, he uttered the immortal words: *'The ball doesn't know the score!'*. In other words, by concentrating only on what he could control (e.g. keeping his head steady as he addressed the ball), Nicklaus remained 'task focused' not 'result focused'. He did not think about what might happen if he missed the putt, but instead used 'trigger words' like 'steady head' to remind him of what to do in that situation. He replaced a negative thought with a positive action. In this way, he showed that the ability to focus on one job at a time, rather than speculating about the possible result of that job, is the secret of effective concentration. But this advice may be difficult to follow because of the fragility of our concentration system.

Why do we lose our concentration? Understanding distractions

People often say 'I lost my concentration'. But have you ever wondered where it actually *went*? Surely it cannot have disappeared altogether? Psychologists have discovered that we never really *lose* our concentration – we merely *re-direct* it to a target which is not relevant to the job we are currently performing. For example, when we encounter difficulty in writing an essay or report, we may switch our attention to an easier and more rewarding task – such as making coffee. Therefore, distractions are events (e.g. an unexpected visitor) and experiences (e.g. feeling anxious) which divert us from our intended thoughts or actions and make it difficult to focus on the job at hand.

In general, there are two types of distractions: external and internal (Moran, 1996). External distractions consist of environmental factors which tend to upset our concentration. These factors include being interrupted by noise or by other people. Although we cannot usually alter them (as they are largely outside our control), we *can* change how we react to them. For example, instead of reacting angrily to noisy members of your family when you are trying to study, you could choose a quieter location in which to work or else request them to remain quiet for agreed periods. Remember that you always have a *choice* about how to respond to any distraction. By contrast, internal distractions are self-generated concerns which arise from our own thoughts and feelings. Typical examples in this category include worrying about what other people might say or do, wondering about the result of tasks long before we complete them, being self-conscious, regretting the past, and feeling tired or bored. In each of these cases, our concentration beam has reversed direction – switching *away* from the task at hand and *towards* internal targets which are irrelevant to the challenge facing us. Fortunately there is a solution to the problem of self-generated distractions. As we can only think of one thing at a time, we have to ensure that what we are thinking about is specific, relevant and under our control. In this way, we can learn to replace distracting thoughts with constructive *actions*. Instead of worrying about what other people might think if you fail an exam next month, it is better to give yourself a specific study task to perform right now. If you can learn to focus only on the present, the future will look after itself. At this stage, however, it may be helpful to explore some possible sources of distraction in your life.

Common distractions affecting students

Here is a list of common distractions which students report. Please read each one carefully and assess the degree to which it affects your studies at present.

- Having so many things to do that you don't know where to start

- Not having a specific goal or question when studying

- Not working to a plan or a timetable

- Feeling too tired to concentrate

- Being interrupted constantly by other people

- Not being able to put personal problems out of your mind

- Thinking too far ahead

- Regretting what happened in the past

- Thinking of unrelated matters while working on a job

- Finding it hard to motivate yourself to begin a task

Most students are thoroughly familiar with these distractions. In fact, hardly a day goes past without encountering at least one of them. But successful students realise that it's not the actual distraction that matters – it is how we *react* to it that affects our learning.

Dealing with distractions

The best way to deal with a distraction is to ensure that it does not arise in the first place. So here are some practical suggestions to prevent yourself from being distracted in study situations.

• Keep your desk as a work-place not a storage place

• Making a start gets you into the mood for studying – don't wait for inspiration to strike

• To avoid fatigue, always set a starting time and a finishing time for your study sessions

• Turn your worries into action-steps (jobs which you can do right now to improve your situation)

• Try to rehearse in your mind exactly what you wish to do next by making a daily job-list of study tasks and check your progress every night

• Take regular exercise (e.g. a walk in the evening) to clear your mind

• Find a quiet place where you know that you will be able to study without being disturbed

• Give yourself visible reminders to re-focus on what is most important right now

In summary, concentration resembles a beam of light which we shine on things which interest us. And when our mental spotlight is directed at what is most important in a given situation, we are 'focused'. In other words, what we are thinking about is the same as what we are doing at that moment. Unfortunately, this focused state of mind is elusive. Thus we often lose our concentration because we allow ourselves to be distracted by external factors (e.g. noise) or by internal concerns (e.g. thinking too far ahead). In both cases, the way in which we react to the distraction is more important than the distraction itself. I suggested some simple tips on dealing with distractions, but blocking out a distraction does not guarantee effective concentration. Additional mental effort is required to focus properly. In the final section of this chapter, I shall explain a set of concentration techniques which should help you to improve your ability to study.

Practical concentration techniques

Most of the following concentration techniques (see Figure 1) are based on methods used by leading athletes to achieve an optimal focus for their performance (Moran, 1996).

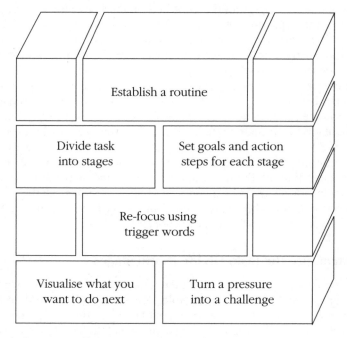

Fig. 1 Concentration Techniques

In this state of mind, there is no difference between what the performer is thinking and what s/he is doing. The techniques below are therefore designed to train you to think only about that which is specific, relevant and under your control.

Establish a routine

Have you ever noticed that many sport stars tend to follow a consistent preparatory routine before they perform their skills? Top tennis players like to bounce the ball a standard number of times before serving and expert golfers like to take a consistent number of practice swings before each shot. This behaviour is not accidental. Instead, it arises from the idea that pre-performance routines remind athletes to focus only on actions that are under their control. Each step of the routine takes them closer to the state of mind in which they perform best. So by using routines, athletes learn to perform at their own pace and to ignore distractions. To illustrate, consider the systematic way in which the Welsh rugby international Neil Jenkins prepares for important kicks: 'I just try and make sure that everything I do on the training ground is repeated on the big day: the angle of the ball, the steps, the strike – and when you do that, it's not that hard to block the crowd out of your mind' (cited in Shalvey, 1995, p. 25).

From such an example we learn that there is a strong connection between the way in which you prepare for a task and how well you will perform it. In other words, a *prepared* mind is a focused one. And the best way to prepare for your studies is to develop a consistent routine for your work. For example, have you ever noticed how difficult it is to concentrate for the first five minutes of a study session? The problem here is that the mind requires a settling-in period and it is during this time that displacement activities (see Chapter 2) will seem most alluring. But if you adhere to a routine, initial distractions will soon fade away. As I explained in Chapter 2, studying at the same time every day enables you to build up a consistent learning habit which will cocoon you from distractions.

Restructure the task: Divide it into stages

Many tasks appear to be difficult merely because of the way in which they are *presented* to us. For example, how is it possible to add up all the numbers between 1 and 1000 in your head (see Box 7.1, Chapter 7, p. 86)? As you will learn, research suggests that the way in which we organise (or 'represent') a problem in our minds affects the speed and efficiency with which we solve it. And since it is usually easier to focus on a small, immediate task rather than a larger, more distant one, it makes sense to restructure problems simply by dividing them into stages. Consider the task of conducting a research assignment (see also Chapter 9). The trick here is to redefine the problem so that every time you sit down to work on it you can make some progress. In this way, you are tackling the problem *on your terms* – not on someone else's assumptions. Put differently, restructuring makes a task more manageable. For example, when writing an essay, you can 'divide and conquer' by considering such sub-problems as: What specific questions underlie the title of this essay? Why are these questions important and for whom do they matter? What headings should I use in my introduction in order to explain the background to this topic? What is the most logical sequence for these headings? What tentative conclusions can I suggest at this stage (to be revised later)?

Set goals and action steps for each stage of your work

Students often lose their concentration because they lack clear questions, objectives or priorities. In Chapter 5, we learned that if you try to read a book without having a specific study question, your mind will soon begin to wander. Similarly, if you go to a lecture or meeting without some idea of what you wish to gain from it, then you are wasting valuable time. To overcome this lack of direction, some form of goal-setting is required (see pp. 20–2). As I explained in Chapter 2, the former Olympic champion swimmer Kieren Perkins said that self-set performance goals (e.g. achieving a personal best time) helped him better than did 'result' goals (e.g. winning the world championship). In this regard, the most productive goals to concentrate on are those which concern immediate actions. Instead of saying 'I'd like to study some time tonight', you should say 'I'll go to the library right now'. Even a question like 'What are my objectives in tackling this problem?' or 'What is my most important goal?' will help you to concentrate on the task at hand.

Use trigger words to re-focus your mind regularly

Our concentration system is rather fragile because our minds were not designed to pay attention to any single source of information for very long. Given this principle, we need some way of *re-focusing* periodically to remind us of our priorities. We can therefore use trigger words or key phrases to point our concentration beam in the right direction whenever we are engaged in a time-consuming task. In Chapter 10, I shall provide some advice on how to re-focus during examinations so that you do not get carried away by irrelevant trains of thought. Some students find 'trigger phrases' such as 'One step at a time', 'Do it now' or 'Keep it going' to be useful reminders of what to do next.

Visualise what you want to do next

The fifth concentration technique involves mental rehearsal or visualisation. Using this technique, people see and feel themselves performing a desired action in their imagination before they actually do it. For example, Martin Hayes, the famous Irish traditional musician, revealed that 'on the days we're doing gigs, I'd visualise the venue all through the day; see myself sitting on stage. That's the whole focus of the day, the gig . . . It's important to focus' (cited in Boland, 1999). A major benefit of this concentration technique is that it provides a feeling that the performer has 'been there before' and will execute the task successfully.

By using our mind's eye, we are turning our mental spotlight on what we want to do or achieve rather than on what might go wrong. In the guided imagery exercise in Box 6.1, you can learn to use your imagination in a constructive manner. The next step is to apply this skill to everyday life. Can you think of a difficult academic situation

---

Box 6.1 *Using visualisation as a concentration technique*

In the following session I am going to take you through a simple visualisation exercise using as many of the senses as possible. Later you can use the same techniques to visualise a positive scene of your own. Before we begin, however, I would like you to make sure that you will not be disturbed for the next few moments. Make sure that you're sitting in a comfortable position, free from distractions. Read carefully the following guided imagery exercise which requires you to imagine travelling through your house.

Make sure that you're sitting in a relaxed position and breathing slowly and regularly. Try to empty your mind of all distractions and concentrate on seeing your house in your mind's eye. Imagine standing in front of your house or apartment on a sunny day. Look up and try to count the number of windows that are visible. Is there a reflection from the sun on the glass? Now, point to each window you can see and count the total number silently to yourself. Walk slowly up the drive way. What can you see on the left and on the right of your path? Try to hear the sound of your feet as you walk up to your front door. Look at the door and notice its colour and texture. Now, take out your door-key from your pocket. Feel the weight and coldness of the key in your hand and notice how it slides gently into the lock. Turn the key slowly and feel the door opening. If you have an alarm, you'd better turn it off as it's beeping in high-pitched tones. Is the hall light on or off? Now, make sure the front door is closed behind you. Take off your coat, hang it up and walk slowly into your kitchen. Walk over to a cupboard and take down an empty glass. Then, turn on the tap and fill the glass with cool water. Turn off the tap, sit down and drink the glass of water slowly. Notice how cool and refreshing it tastes. Next, walk over to the sink, rinse the glass and leave it aside. Then, walk out of the kitchen and into your living-room. Sit down in your favourite chair or sofa and feel yourself begin to relax completely. You're happy to be home.

which you will face shortly? This situation could involve standing up in front of your class to make a presentation on a specific topic or it could be an oral examination which you have to take. Now, try to 'see' and 'feel' this situation in your mind's eye. Visualise all the actions that you wish to perform in this challenging situation. For example, imagine speaking slowly and confidently to your class, illustrating ideas using your slides or overhead transparencies. Notice how calm and confident you are in this imaginary situation. Finally, try to replay this image in your mind – over and over again.

Turn pressure into a challenge

Pressure is experienced whenever we react with fear to an event or situation that threatens to overwhelm us in some way. One of the most important mental skills possessed by top-class sport performers is the ability to stay *calm* and *focused* in pressure situations (e.g. when taking a penalty in the last minute of a cup-final or when facing a five feet golf putt on the 18th green). How is this possible when it seems more natural to worry about the consequences of failure in such situations – especially when fame and fortune may be at stake? Briefly, research suggests that the way in which we *perceive* a pressure situation determines how well we perform in it. Specifically, the objective facts of any situation can be interpreted as either a *threat* or a *challenge* – depending on how we look at it. To explain, if we focus on what might happen if we fail, we end up distracting ourselves by thinking about future results rather than what we have to do right now. This 'threat response' makes us anxious because we inevitably imagine failure rather than success. But if we concentrate instead on the specific challenge posed by the current situation (the immediate job that needs to be done), we begin to adopt a helpful performance focus. Therefore, the 'challenge response' helps us to think only about actions that are under our control. Consistent winners in business and sport have been trained to see the *challenge* (or opportunity) rather than the *threat* in any difficult situations which they encounter. Consider this quote from the famous golfer Jack Nicklaus. 'Sure, you're nervous', he said, 'but that's the difference between being able to win and not being able to win. And that's the fun of it, to put yourself into the position of being nervous, being excited. I never look at it as pressure. I look on it as fun and excitement' (cited in Gilleece, 1996, p. 7). That's fine in sport – but how can we apply this 'challenge response' to your studies? Try Box 6.2.

| Box 6.2 | *Turning pressure into a challenge* |

Think of a pressure situation in your academic work at present and use it to complete the following sentence.

(i) *'I hate the pressure of . . .'*

For example, it could be 'I hate the pressure of not knowing what is going to be asked in an examination'.

Now pause for a moment and try to turn this source of pressure into a challenge by finishing the sentence below

(ii) *'I love the challenge of . . .'*

This time, you could say: 'I love the challenge of working through questions from last year's examination'.

Notice that sentence (ii) specifies actions that are specific, relevant and under your control whereas sentence (i) focuses only on worries. The lesson to be learned here is that pressures can become challenges if you focus only on the job to be done right now.

In summary, the best way to remain calm and focused under pressure is to turn a difficult situation into a challenge to your abilities. By 'framing' a pressure situation in this way, you are learning to focus only on *actions that lie under your control*. In other words, the challenge response brings out your best qualities whereas the pressure response brings out your greatest fears. Remember that you always have a choice in the way in which you perceive situations. So, psychologically, we see things *when* we believe them – not the other way around. Therefore, pressure lies in the mind of the beholder. So which perception will you choose to act on – pressure or challenge?

Summary

Concentration, or the ability to focus on what is most important in any situation while ignoring distractions, is a vital skill in everyday life (whether in studying, business or in competitive sport). Unfortunately, most of us are more familiar with lapses of attention (e.g. when we find ourselves absent-mindedly reading the same sentence in a book over and over again because our thoughts are 'miles away') than with those rare moments of intense absorption (focused states) when there is no difference between what we are thinking and what we are doing. Therefore, this chapter set out to explore such questions as: What is concentration? Why do we lose it so easily? And what practical techniques can we use to improve our ability to 'focus' more effectively in academic situations? In the first section, I likened concentration to a mental spotlight which we shine at things in which we are interested. In other words, concentration is 'interest in action'. And we focus best when what we are thinking about is specific, relevant and under our control. Anything else is likely to distract us. Unfortunately, this happens whenever we allow something (e.g. unwanted noise or perhaps a worry about the *result* of what we are doing) to divert our mental spotlight from its intended target. But as I explained, it's not what happens to us – but how we *think* about and *react* to it that affects our concentration. For example, studying with the radio on may not bother you unduly – provided that you are in control of its volume. But this noise may prove distracting if *someone else* turned it on or is in control of it. In the final section of the chapter, I presented a set of practical techniques which can improve your concentration and help you to study more efficiently. These techniques included establishing study routines, dividing study tasks into stages, setting action goals for your work, using trigger words to re-focus regularly, visualising what you want to do next and turning sources of pressure or worry into enjoyable challenges (by focusing only on actions that are specific, relevant and under your control).

7. Learning to Think Critically: The Importance of Being Sceptical

'Thinking is natural, but unfortunately, critical thinking is not' (Walsh & Paul, 1986, p. 13)

'Many people would sooner die than think. In fact, they do' (Bertrand Russell, quoted in Collins, 1996).

'Baloney, bamboozles, bunk, careless thinking, flimflam and wishes disguised as facts are not restricted to parlour magic and ambiguous advice on matters of the heart. Unfortunately, they ripple through mainstream political, social, religious and economic issues in every nation' (Sagan, 1987, p. 13).

'We have an irrational veneration for the media. If we read something in a book or newspaper, or hear it on the radio, or see it on TV, we assume it must be true unless we have personal experience to the contrary' (Lee, 1996, p. 16).

Introduction

Some years ago, one of my research students conducted a study on the smoking habits of university students. This study attracted national publicity and after the student had been interviewed by a press reporter, the following headline appeared in a daily newspaper: '*Smoking more common than thought in UCD!*' Although the unintentional ambiguity of this statement raises some comical questions (are students too burnt out to think?), there is a serious issue at stake here. Specifically, have our thinking habits declined as a result of the amount of information which assails us every day? Lee (1996) believes so when he suggests that 'it is high time we began to learn consciously how to begin decoding the barrage of information with which we are all daily bombarded' (p. 16). But how do we go about sharpening our judgement? Perhaps the best solution is to train people in critical thinking skills so that they will not only ask the right questions – but also be able to evaluate appropriate answers. As McGuinness (1996) suggests, 'if we want people to become life-long learners, then we must enable them . . . to learn to think' (p. 1). The purpose of this chapter, therefore, is to explain how you can improve your ability to think critically.

To do this, I shall proceed as follows. First, I shall explore thinking as a mental skill by which we make sense of the world (including ourselves and other people). Next, I shall explain the importance of critical thinking or the ability to form independent conclusions by evaluating available evidence and arguments on any given topic. Finally, I shall present a range of questions and techniques which are designed to improve your ability to think critically about what you learn.

Thinking: The skill of making sense of things

We are born with a desire to understand or to make sense of the world. We do this initially by noticing the consequences of what we do. For example, as infants, we discover the basic laws of gravity – not by reading physics books or by listening to our parents but by throwing objects out of prams and by observing how and where they fall! When we learn to speak, we ask questions of everyone we meet. Then, after we go to school and learn to read, we use *books* to gain access to other people's knowledge and experience. At this stage, our ability to write helps us to externalise, and hence clarify, our thinking. But what exactly is thinking?

For psychologists, thinking is a mental (or cognitive) process through which we attempt to understand things by using our knowledge and imagination to go beyond what is immediately apparent or to see how situations could be different. For example, the fact that you may notice that there is furniture in your room does not involve any thinking – merely sensory registration. But imagining what your room would look like *if your furniture were re-arranged* involves a cognitive leap beyond the obvious which constitutes thinking. And the wonder of this skill is that it allows us to *transform* a situation mentally – to play with it in our heads. But what do we think *about*? The short answer is – knowledge. More precisely, thinking is what happens when our mind manipulates what we know, or can imagine, in order to transform a situation. In other words, we *restructure* our knowledge whenever we think about something.

To experience restructuring at first hand, please try the exercise in Box 7.1. In this exercise, you will discover the importance of restructuring a problem in order to solve it. As you will see, Gauss detected a pattern in the numbers and used his imagination to re-organise the problem so that a creative solution popped out. But in what sense is this type of thinking skilful?

| Box 7.1 | The power of thinking: Restructuring a problem |

Creative thinkers can use their knowledge to restructure a problem rapidly in their minds. To illustrate, consider the following puzzle. What is the sum of all whole numbers between 1 and 1000?

The obvious (and long-winded) way to solve this problem is to write down all the numbers from 1 to 1000 and add them up. Although this solution will work, it is cumbersome, time-consuming and susceptible to error. Fortunately, there is a much simpler way of tackling this task – a strategy which was discovered after a moment's creative thought by a young mathematical genius called Carl Friedrich Gauss who had been presented with this problem by his teacher in school. Here is what happened.

Step 1 *Gauss began by 'representing' the problem on paper in the conventional way:*

$$1 + \ldots + 1000$$

Step 2 *Then, he looked at the problem again, paused for reflection and restructured it like this:*

$$1 + 2 + 3 \ldots + 998 + 999 + 1000$$

Step 3 *Next, he wrote down 1+1000 and then 2+999. Suddenly, he announced the solution to his teacher: 500,500.*

Can you work out how he solved this puzzle so quickly? How did restructuring help him to establish the correct answer? (See p. 100)

Most people agree that physical activities such as typing, swimming and driving are skills because they involve learned behaviour which can be improved through instruction and practice. But how could a mental activity like *thinking* be regarded as a skill? Well, if we define a skill as any action, physical or mental, which is goal-directed, organised and acquired through training and practice (Annett, 1991), then certain kinds of thinking (e.g. reasoning) could be deemed skilful. And if thinking is a skill, then people vary in their ability to use it effectively. So, now we need to consider the nature and importance of critical thinking in our daily lives.

What is critical thinking?

Every day, we are faced with a variety of complex and controversial questions. For example, is abortion right or wrong? Should certain drugs be legalised? Unfortunately, as weighing up the evidence on these questions is hard work, it is not surprising that we sometimes take short cuts by accepting other people's opinions on these matters without question. In this 'mindless' state, we resemble sponges because we soak up knowledge indiscriminately (see also Chapter 4). This blunting of our questioning and judging skills is exacerbated by certain design flaws in our minds – such as the fact that our working (or short-term) memory system is brief and fragile (e.g. we cannot keep track of things in our minds for more than 30 seconds without deliberate rehearsal; see also Chapter 8) and that conditional reasoning (or 'if-then' logic) is difficult both to perform and to comprehend. One way of overcoming these limitations, however, is to use questions which get to the heart of the matter. As you can see from Box 7.2, questioning activates many useful cognitive operations.

Box 7.2   *Asking questions to promote critical thinking*

Question	Cognitive operation activated
What are the key features of. . . ?	Analysis
What is the main assumption underlying. . . ?	Analysis
What are the strengths and weaknesses of. . . ?	Evaluation
What do you already know about. . . ?	Prior knowledge accessed
In what ways are X and Y similar?	Analogical thinking
What do you think would happen if. . . ?	Prediction
What is the evidence to support. . . ?	Logical
What is a good example of. . . ?	Application
What is the key idea. . . ?	Inference
Can you think of another way of looking at . . . ?	Creativity

Asking questions and looking for evidence are the keys to critical thinking

Using questions such as those in Box 7.2 promotes a mental sharpness which underlies all forms of critical thinking. But what does this term really mean?

Critical thinking may be defined as a form of intelligent criticism which helps people to reach independent and justifiable conclusions about their experiences. According to Bernstein, Clarke-Stewart, Penner, Roy & Wickens (2000), it is the ability to assess claims and make judgements on the basis of well-supported evidence. What makes this form of thinking especially valuable is that it is based on *active reflection* (i.e. working things out for oneself) rather than on passive reproduction of other people's ideas. For example, when my brother, Dermot, was six years old, he came home one day and informed my mother that he had severe doubts about his teacher's ability. Naturally, my mother probed the reason for this opinion. 'Well', Dermot replied, 'he gave us a spelling test today and told us to close our books – but he kept *his* book open, so he mustn't have known the spellings himself!'. Although Dermot's conclusion was not the only one warranted by the evidence available, there is no doubt that he had shown a precocious ability to think critically about an everyday situation. Perhaps not surprisingly, he subsequently became a philosophy professor. As you can see, critical thinking is characterised by a *rational evaluation* of available evidence. Accordingly, it involves two key components – a sceptical attitude and a toolbox of reasoning skills.

The attitudinal part of critical thinking consists of a willingness to question what you learn. For example, what evidence do people offer in support of their conclusions? And is this evidence valid and relevant? Clearly, questions of this nature (see the next section of this chapter) stem from adopting a *sceptical attitude* towards any claims which we are requested to believe (e.g. the astrological proposition that our star sign influences our behaviour in predictable ways). This sceptical attitude contrasts sharply with the mindlessness and passivity which characterises some of our everyday actions (e.g. when we turn to syndicated astrological columns in the newspaper for advice on our lives). But questioning on its own does not sharpen our thinking. We also need to be able to assess rationally the plausibility of the answers which our questions elicit. And this requires the ability to spot errors and inconsistencies in the evidence and arguments which underlie what we are asked to believe. Therefore, in the next section, I shall provide a toolbox of questions and techniques which should help to improve your ability to think critically.

Developing your ability to think critically

Although the ability to think for oneself has long been championed as a major goal of a third-level education (e.g. see Dewey, 1933), little or no concern has been devoted to practical ways of producing this skill. This neglect is due, in part, to a widespread belief that effective thinking will develop as a spontaneous by-product of learning such subjects as computing or mathematics. In other words, teaching people *what* to think is assumed to train them *how* to think as well. Unfortunately, there is little evidence to support this assumption. A more direct approach to the problem of teaching thinking skills has emerged of late in which people are being taught to ask certain types of questions in order to analyse an argument or to evaluate relevant evidence (see review by McGuinness, 1996). By asking such questions, people become *systematically* inquisitive or sceptical. And scepticism, which comes from the Greek word *skeptomai* (which means 'I consider thoughtfully'), is the essence of critical thinking. So what questions should you ask in order to think critically about what you learn? The following guideline is based on checklists proposed by Browne & Keeley (1994), Roediger *et al.* (1995) and Shermer (1997).

What exactly is the claim or conclusion that I am asked to believe?

The first step in critical thinking is to identify the claim or conclusion that you are being asked to believe. This task is usually quite easy because authors often *tell you* explicitly what conclusion they would like you to accept by including this information in the sub-title, preface or conclusion of their work (e.g. 'Emotional Intelligence: *Why It Can Matter More Than IQ*' – note the sub-title which I have italicised). But what if you can't *find* such information? In this case, you will have to infer it from the text. But sometimes, this process of inferring the claim can be hazardous. For example, consider how advertisers overcome the prohibition on making false statements in their publicity by encouraging you to draw conclusions which support their claims. If you were told that 'nine out of ten doctors recommend the pain relieving ingredient in Hangover Tablets', should you conclude that these tablets are effective? Not necessarily. Why? Because the advertisers have neglected to inform you that the *same* ingredient is common to most painkilling tablets. In other words, the medical endorsement is for the *generic ingredient* – not for the new tablets. (By the way, in a satirical reference to such advertisements, the Irish comedian Dylan Moran once quipped that two out of three people spend a lot of time wondering what happened to the third person!)

Who/what is the source of the claim(s)?

When assessing a claim or an argument, it is important to establish *the credibility of the source* of this information. The reason for this step is that not all sources are equally trustworthy or impartial. You should, for example, be cautious about accepting the claims of people who do not have any special competence in a relevant field or who appear to be endorsing a particular view purely for personal gain. Likewise, you should be sceptical of research reports publicised by organisations which possess a vested interest in certain conclusions (e.g. tobacco companies may announce that they have discovered that there are no risks of cancer from smoking cigarettes). Also related to source credibility is the problem of over-reliance on second-hand information. To explain, a variety of biases and distortions can occur when the 'facts' of a story are dependent on secondary sources. For example, consider the prevalence of urban myths in our lives. These myths are fictitious stories, usually carrying a moral message, which are related as allegedly true events. Typical characters in these stories are cats in microwave ovens, mysterious hitchhikers, vengeful AIDS victims and burglars who terrorise babysitters! Interestingly, these stories are found in all cultures and have criss-crossed the globe for many years. One such apocryphal tale concerns a philosophy examination in which a student, when presented with a question 'Why?' simply wrote down 'Why not?' and allegedly got full marks!

Interestingly, myths can become a part of scientific folklore. Consider the case of 'subliminal advertising' or the presentation of messages which, although below the threshold of our conscious awareness, may be registered by our minds. Many people have some vague knowledge of research in the US which purported to show that subliminal messages like 'eat popcorn' or 'buy Coke' could affect the behaviour of cinema audiences exposed unwittingly to them. Unfortunately, there is no evidence that such research was ever conducted (see Roediger *et al.*, 1995). Apparently, this story became an urban myth simply because it was 'too good to be false'! Some other scientific myths in this vein are described in Box 7.3.

Box 7.3	*Don't believe everything you read in books! Eskimos, snow and the '10%-of-your-brain' myth.*

You should not believe everything that you read in textbooks. Authors make mistakes due to a combination of two main problems – laziness and unconscious distortion. By laziness, I mean a tendency to rely too much on second-hand sources of information (material reported in other textbooks) rather than on original data. And unconscious distortion refers to the process by which some authors unwittingly alter a finding in order to make it compatible with their favourite theories. To illustrate these problems, consider two scientific myths – the popular claim that we use only about 10% of our brains and the theory that Eskimos have more words for snow than do native speakers of English.

The claim that we use only '10%-of-our-brains' is intriguing for at least three reasons. First, it has been promulgated by a wide variety of famous people ranging from Dale Carnegie (of *How to Win Friends and Influence People* fame) to Albert Einstein. Second, nobody seems to be know what the claim means precisely (McBurney, 1996). On the one hand, it could mean that we can do without 90% of our brains! Alternatively, it may indicate that we could do 10 times better in mental tasks if we tried harder. Unfortunately, the claim is not specified precisely enough to be testable. Finally, little or no evidence is cited to support it. Indeed, according to Beyerstein (1999), this claim originated from a mis-understanding among brain researchers in the 1930s. To explain, on the basis that specific functions had been identified for less than *one-eighth* of the brain at that time, it was suggested that we used less than 10% of this organ. However, current neurological research suggests that this speculation is false as vast areas of the brain are active during the performance of even the most trivial of mental tasks (Sternberg, 1999). Therefore, it is simply *not true* that most of the brain is idle as we go about our mundane chores. If so, why is this '10% myth' so tenacious? Perhaps its enduring appeal is rooted in our willingness to believe that we all have skills and talents that remain untapped – a reservoir of potential that could overflow into our humdrum lives (Beyerstein, 1999). In other words, it may suit us to believe 'the 10% myth' because it suggests that the difference between mediocrity and genius is simply the proportion of our brain cells that is active at any given moment!

Another myth concerns the 'Eskimo vocabulary hoax' (Pullum, 1991). Briefly, according to linguistic relativity theory, speakers of different languages *think* differently because of differences in the way in which they carve up the world linguistically, or make distinctions between things. For example, because Burmese rice-farmers have more terms for the word rice than we do, it seems possible that they think about it differently from the way in which we think of rice. Similarly, it is often alleged that Eskimos (or, more correctly, the Inuit people) have more words for snow than do native speakers of English. Indeed, over the years, the number of such words has grown from nine to four hundred (Pinker, 1994)! This example is so vivid and compelling that it is rarely questioned – even though it is untrue (Martin, 1986). Just as in the case of subliminal advertising, the Eskimo example is too good to be false!

In order to counteract distortions arising from the biasing effect of second-hand information, Gilovich (1991) recommends that our scepticism should be in *direct proportion* to the remoteness of the source of the claim in question. In other words, the more distant the source, the less credible is the story which emanates from it. Accordingly, whenever possible, you should consult *primary sources* (i.e. the original book or article by a certain author) to validate claims encountered in secondary sources such as textbooks.

What evidence is used to support the main argument or central claim(s)?

The information which bombards us every day stems from a variety of sources which range from intuitive hunches (e.g. your first impressions of a character in a novel) to more objective data (e.g. that from controlled laboratory experiments). Unfortunately, these sources of information are not equally trustworthy. For example, a major problem with insights yielded by intuitive impressions (or gut reactions) is that they are invariably based on a limited sample of experience. For example, a single media report of a spectacular airplane crash might cause you to overestimate the danger of travelling by air – even though, statistically, you may be much more likely to die in a car-crash or in your sleep!

A list of some common sources of evidence which you may encounter in your studies is presented in Box 7.4.

Box 7.4 *Common sources of evidence cited in arguments*

Intuition (gut feeling)
A private feeling or 'hunch' which may be used both to make and to justify judgements and decisions.

Appeal to authority
Ascribing a claim (e.g. a quotation) or argument to an apparently prestigious source (the expert authority) in an effort to enhance its credibility or persuasive appeal.

Anecdotal evidence
Includes reference to personal experiences such as observations, case-studies and/or examples.

Research evidence
Comprises data obtained through systematic, objective and repeatable procedures (e.g. a controlled laboratory experiment).

Although space limitations preclude a detailed analysis of all of this evidence, the use of case studies deserves special attention. For example, critics of the legal system may try to highlight the inequities of sentencing policy by presenting vivid examples of offenders who received disproportionately severe punishments for petty crimes. But although such case studies can provide compelling insights which resonate with our experience, they are highly selective in nature and hence susceptible to many biases (e.g. how can we be sure that the case-study is representative of the population from which it comes?). Therefore, when we encounter a case-study, we should be careful to ask questions about sampling, generalisability and the possible existence of any *counter examples* which may challenge the conclusions presented to us.

How valid is the evidence cited? Becoming an efficient consumer of research information

Having identified the foundations supporting the conclusions on offer, the next step is to evaluate this evidence systematically. Doing this is important because you will be expected to become a shrewd and efficient consumer of research information in university. This means that you will have to become adept at making quick judgements about the validity and reliability of the information cited in support of the persuasive appeals to which you will be subjected. This task is manageable if you have been trained to identify potential flaws and inconsistencies in arguments (including your own, of course!). Here are five points to note (see also Bransford & Stein, 1984; Foegelin & Sinnott-Armstrong, 1991).

First, a claim may be based on inaccurate information. For example, consider the widespread belief that spinach is unusually rich in iron. Apparently, this belief is mistaken. Indeed, research suggests that there is more iron in eggs, liver, brown sugar or pulses than in spinach (Skrabanek & McCormick, 1989). Interestingly, this myth arose from research conducted in the late 1890s and served as a useful propaganda weapon for the Allied Forces during the Second World War when meat was rationed. Indeed, according to Hamblin (1981), evidence has existed since the 1930s to show that the original researchers who had investigated the iron content of spinach had put the decimal point in the wrong place, thereby overestimating the resulting value tenfold! Unfortunately, this error has passed into folklore and fiction has been promulgated as truth. The lesson is that many of our most cherished beliefs have not been subjected to critical scrutiny.

A second common flaw afflicting arguments occurs when the authors use invalid reasoning processes. Imagine that you are a scientist who has received criticism for your theory that extrasensory perception (ESP) exists. In a public debate on this topic, you produce the following argument. As some currently accepted scientific theories were originally regarded as being false (e.g. Pasteur's idea that diseases were transmitted by germs that were too small to be seen by the naked eye; Galileo dismissing Kepler's idea that the moon exerts an influence on ocean tides), and since *your* theory has been ridiculed by the scientific community, then your theory must, in fact, be true. Is this argument valid? Of course not, but it could convince some people that your ideas are correct.

A third weakness of many arguments concerns shaky foundations or questionable assumptions. This problem is especially likely when figurative language is used because metaphors always carry implicit assumptions with them when they are imported into arguments or theories. For example, in Chapter 8, I criticise the traditional model of the long-term memory system as a container which, when filled beyond its capacity, overflows. Although this model seems plausible, on the basis of everyday experience, it is actually false. Thus research shows that there is no known limit to our long-term memory. Indeed, our memory *expands* to accommodate the knowledge which it receives. In short, the more we know, the more we can remember!

A fourth way in which arguments can be misleading occur when claims are made which, regardless of their truth value, have *no bearing* on the central point. For example, an Irish demagogue of the last century once accused a political adversary of being 'a practising *homo sapiens*'! This is an illustration of an *ad hominem* remark, or a disparaging comment on the character or motives of a rival, rather than a reasoned attack on the issue at stake. Another example of a fallacy of relevance arises occasionally when the 'wrong' experts are brought in to lend authority or support to a position. Consider the controversy over the alleged psychic abilities of certain people. In particular, let's focus on the incident in which Uri Geller demonstrated his apparent ability to bend spoons, by mental power alone, in front of an expert panel of scientists. A curious feature of this case was neither the actual spoon-bending (which has been replicated many times by the stage magician and psychic debunker, James Randi; see Randi, 1975), nor the fact that scientists could be fooled by an expert magician. Instead, what surprised commentators was the fact that the scientists in question had assumed that they had sufficient expertise to assess whether or not Geller's demonstration was 'paranormal'. As Foegelin & Sinnott-Armstrong (1991) point out, why did these scientists not try to rule out a 'normal' explanation of mental spoon-bending first by asking Geller to perform in front of a panel of expert magicians? As a useful rule of thumb, it is unwise to believe any claim for which the only supporting evidence is an appeal to authority.

A fifth flaw in arguments concerns 'fallacies of vacuity'. These arise when an argument is circular (when the same statement is used both as a premise and a conclusion) or when it 'begs the question' (by including a premise which pre-supposes the point at issue). An example of circular reasoning is when a person's inability to read is attributed to a reading problem, which is then regarded as a cause of the behaviour in question. Begging the question means taking the conclusion for granted. For example, imagine a barrister in a courtroom asking a witness to a robbery: 'Was the gun in the man's left hand or right hand?' Obviously, this question assumes that the man had a gun in the first place. Likewise, an example of an argument which begs the question is one which states that 'The age of sexual responsibility should be lowered to fifteen because fifteen-year-olds are mature enough to have sex'. You should always be suspicious of circular reasoning and question-begging whenever the evidence is a re-statement of the conclusion.

In summary, all sources of evidence have their limitations. Therefore, you might find it helpful to examine Box 7.5 so that you will know what to look for when you are required to evaluate evidence in your subject.

Let's look at some of the sources of evidence described in Box 7.5. Perhaps the most frequently used one is the 'appeal to authority'. Here, testimonials or endorsements may be given by people who are acknowledged authority figures in a particular field. For example, a leading heart surgeon or world-class athlete may be quoted on the cardiovascular benefits of regular exercise. But should we readily accept what these eminent people have said about this topic? Well, as critical thinkers, we should immediately look for evidence to support any conclusions which we are offered. To do this, we should check whether or not the expert involved has any specialist knowledge in the field in question. For example, a Nobel Prizewinner's views on his or her subject are presumably better informed than those of somebody unknown in this field. However, if no evidence is adduced to support this person's position, or if the expert's pronouncement lies outside his or her domain of expertise (a trick which is exploited repeatedly in advertising), then his/her opinions must be treated with scepticism. Some useful internet addresses to help you to exercise your scepticism are presented at the end of the chapter.

Are there alternative explanations for the evidence provided? If so, how plausible are these rival theories?

What you see depends on the view from where you are standing. In other words, there are always alternative ways of interpreting anything. Indeed, the possibility of identifying rival explanations for an agreed set of circumstances is the cornerstone of our legal system. If a

| Box 7.5 | *How good is the evidence? What to look out for when evaluating explanations* |

Source	**Potential flaw**
Intuition	*Inaccessible to public scrutiny and hence unverifiable.*
Personal experience	*Personal observations ('I saw it with my own eyes') or single episodes, no matter how vivid, do not constitute proof. They are also subject to distortions arising from our attitudes and expectations.*
Expert authority	*The 'expert' involved may be commenting on a topic outside his/her specialist field (in which case, the opinion offered is questionable) or s/he may be doing so for personal gain (e.g. advertising endorsement).*
Case studies	*Examples do not constitute proof. They are also susceptible to selective or biased reporting. Furthermore, the absence of relevant comparative data makes interpretation of case studies difficult.*
Research evidence	*Difficult and time-consuming to obtain.*

defence counsel can prove that there is at least a 'reasonable doubt' about his or her client's involvement in a crime, then the case against this person may be dismissed. By implication, if you can establish an interpretation of the evidence which is at least as plausible as that favoured by the theorist, then you have shown a capacity to think for yourself. Remember, it is this ability to think rigorously which is the hallmark of a First Class Honours answer from a student.

To illustrate the search for 'rival causes', consider the mystery of 'out of the body' (OBE) experiences. These phenomena, which are commonly reported in certain situations (e.g. when close to death), refer to changes in consciousness that are accompanied by a feeling that one's centre of awareness has shifted to a position that is separate from one's body. Now, one possible explanation for these experiences is that they represent proof of the existence of the soul. This is a supernatural explanation of the known facts. However, alternative explanations are possible – natural ones which are compatible with known physical or psychological principles. For example, a good place to start looking for the cause of things is to analyse the situations in which they occur. Interestingly, 90% of OBE experiences tend to be reported when people are lying down (e.g. on a bed, in an operating theatre) in a state of reverie, between wakefulness and sleep. And when people are lying down in a relaxed state, several things can happen. First, being stationary for long periods of time can cause habituation (or shutting off) of the receptors which regulate our body sense. As a result, we may experience a sensation of floating. Second, as we see with our minds rather than with our eyes, OBEs may arise from attempts to make sense of the world using only our imagination. Combining these insights, it seems possible that 'out of the body' experiences may simply occur as incidental consequences of being in a relaxed state for a period of time. This explanation offers an alternative view to the idea that OBEs are proof of reincarnation.

Check your assumptions before drawing conclusions

The final step in learning to think critically is to make sure that you check your assumptions before drawing any conclusions. All too often we ignore this advice and make hasty and unwarranted judgements as a result. To test the sharpness of your thinking in this area, please try the exercise in Box 7.6.

As you can see, Box 7.6 reveals the folly of taking things for granted – the antithesis of critical thinking because it is rooted in passive acceptance rather than in active questioning of the information provided.

Overall, this section presented a set of questions and techniques which are intended to promote intelligent criticism of the information which bombards you every day. Let us now summarise this advice as a practical checklist for your role as a research 'consumer' in the university.

Putting it all together: Becoming a critical reader

During your studies at university, you will be expected to read thousands of books and articles, all of which will try to convince you of the merit of their authority, information or arguments. How can you apply the critical thinking skills that you have learned in this chapter to evaluate this literature thoroughly? Here are some practical guidelines in this regard (based on Bernstein *et al.*, 2000).

- Who is the author? What is the source? Is this source credible?

Box 7.6	*How good are you at checking your assumptions?*

Here are three puzzles for you to solve (based on Bransford & Stein, 1984). The key to solution in each case lies in checking your assumptions carefully.

1. *If a plane crashed on the border between Northern Ireland and the Republic of Ireland, where would the survivors be buried?*

2. *How can you make a tennis ball go a short distance, come to a halt an then reverse itself by going in the opposite direction? You are not allowed to bounce, spin or tie anything to the ball.*

3. *At a party, you meet a woman who can predict perfectly the score of any match, in any sport, before it is played. How is this possible?*

The answers to these questions are on p. 100.

- What is the main idea or general message? What specifically am I asked to believe/accept?

- What specific evidence does the author cite in support of his/her position?

- Is this evidence valid and convincing? If not, what other evidence would I need in order to be satisfied with the conclusions drawn?

- Are there any alternative explanations for the evidence supplied by the author? If so, what are they and what conclusions do they lead to?

- What is the best/most plausible explanation warranted by the evidence available?

- What are the main ideas that have I learned from this book/article?

- How do these ideas/findings fit in with what I already know?

Summary

The capacity to think is so natural that we almost take it for granted. But the ability to think *critically*, or to form independent conclusions based on a rational evaluation of available evidence, requires hard work and special training. Accordingly, it is a highly valued skill which distinguishes truly educated people from those who believe everything that they read or are told. But what does critical thinking involve and how can it be developed practically? These two questions provided the impetus for this chapter. I began by suggesting that thinking is a mental skill by which we make sense of the world (including ourselves and other people). Then, I explained that critical thinking is a form of intelligent criticism which helps us to assess the validity of what we are asked to believe in everyday life. Briefly, it requires both a sceptical attitude (or a willingness to question any claims which we are asked to accept) and a 'toolbox' of reasoning skills (including the ability to identify flaws in evidence and arguments underlying theories we are asked to believe).

In the final section, I provided a set of practical questions and techniques which should help to improve your ability to think critically before jumping to conclusions. These questions showed you how to identify and evaluate the claim at issue, the source of this claim, the evidence adduced in support of it, the validity of relevant evidence, the possibility of alternative explanations and the possible existence of false assumptions underlying the argument(s) under scrutiny. I concluded the chapter by presenting a brief checklist of questions designed to promote intelligent criticism for the sceptical reader.

Here are some internet sites that may help you to evaluate information with appropriate scepticism:

<www.quackwatch.com> A large repository of crackpot therapies and miracle cures that have been debunked scientifically

<urbanlegends.about.com> A catalogue of urban legends, hoaxes and frauds.

<www.snopes.com> a compendium of urban myths

Answer to Box 7.1 (p. 86)

He noticed that there were 500 pairs of numbers which aggregated to 1001. The answer is therefore 500 times 1001.

Answers to Box 7.6 (p. 99)

1. Answer: Nowhere – survivors of a plane-crash do not have to be buried until they are dead! Most people fail to register the meaning of the word 'survivors'.

2. Answer: Toss the ball up in the air and it will do the rest. Most people get stuck on this problem because they assume falsely that the ball should be rolled horizontally rather than tossed vertically.

3. Answer: Anyone can predict the *score* of a match *before* it is played – 0–0!

8. Remembering and Understanding

'Everyone complains of his memory; nobody of his judgement'
(La Rochefoucauld, Duc de, 1678)

Introduction

Let's begin this chapter with a rather unusual request. *Forget* the word 'thunder'. As you will discover, this task is surprisingly difficult because *paying attention* to something is the first step in remembering it. Paradoxically, therefore, trying to forget something can make it even *more* memorable! Interestingly, the plight of a man who had a pathological inability to forget anything was explored by the Argentinian writer Jorge Luis Borges in a short story called *Funes the Memorious* (Borges, 1970). This tale, which was influenced by the author's lifelong struggle with insomnia, describes a fictional character who was cursed with a memory so perfect that he could recall every sight, sound and sensation that he had ever experienced. Imagine the agony that Funes must have experienced when it took him as long to recall events as the events themselves had lasted initially! Despite having some sympathy for the predicament of Funes, however, you probably wish that you had a better memory for academic course material. But is it really your memory that is letting you down at present – or could it be that your *understanding* of what you have to learn is rather faulty? If this question interests you, then this chapter is worth reading because it will provide some practical advice on increasing your ability both to understand and to remember what you learn in university. Accordingly, I shall proceed as follows.

To begin with, I shall explore the nature of memory and the steps involved in remembering anything. Then, I shall explain the structure of the memory system. Next, I shall present five practical techniques which can be used to improve your ability to understand (and hence recall) what you learn. Finally, some mnemonics (memory techniques) to facilitate rote learning (learning off by heart) will be considered. Before we begin, however, I would like to test your ability to remember some numbers (see Box 8.1). Although this exercise is just a trick, it highlights an important principle of memory. Specifically, imposing *organisation* on what you have to learn (e.g. by breaking the information into sub-groups or 'chunks') is a good way of improving your

---

| Box 8.1 | How good is your memory for numbers? |

The purpose of this exercise is to test your memory for numbers. To take part, you will need to have a pen and paper available. Now, have a quick glance at the 24 numbers below. Do you think that you could remember all of them?

1 4 9 1 6 2 5 3 6 4 9 6 4 8 1 1 0 0 1 2 1 1 4 4

Look at the numbers carefully for about ten seconds and then cover them up. Now, without looking at them, try to remember as many of them as possible in the correct sequence.

Most people find this task impossible because 24 items exceed our immediate memory span (which ranges between seven and nine separate units – the length of a typical telephone number). But what happens if you manage to spot a pattern which 'chunks' these numbers into sub-groups? This strategy leads to immediate success because it changes the nature of the memory task. Instead of having to recall 24 separate numbers, all you have to do is to remember one item: the pattern which generates these numbers. Amazingly, knowledge of this rule will enable you to recall the numbers *backwards* as well as forwards! What is the rule? Here's a clue. The pattern has something to do with squares. But if you're still baffled, the solution can be found on p. 117.

---

memory for any kind of material. For example, instead of trying to learn a telephone number (e.g. 2081945) as seven separate digits, you could re-code it mentally using such words as 'twenty', 'eight' and 'nineteen forty-five'. Now, you have to remember only three chunks – one of which (1945) should be lodged in your mind because of its significance in European history. And if you can establish some association between the material to be learned and what you already know (in this case, the end of the Second World War), then your memory will be strengthened. This leads to another vital principle of memory – the more we already *know*, the more we can remember! The implication of this principle is that memory improves with knowledge. In short, the more often you check what you know, the better prepared your memory will be for absorbing new material.

What is memory?

Memory is an active mental system which stores general knowledge (e.g. that Dublin is the capital of Ireland), personal experiences (e.g. our first day in university) and skills (e.g. how to play tennis) over time so that they are available to us later when required. Life without memory would be chaotic. For example, we would not know who or where we were and being unable to link the past with the present, we would be incapable of learning anything. Indeed, without memory, we would not be able to read, write or perform even the simplest of actions as all of these skills depend on rapid access to stored knowledge.

But what kind of storage system is our memory? Although it has been compared with various mechanical devices (filing cabinets, video recorders, computers), the human memory system is unique in its flexibility and sophistication. For example, it is unlike a container or filing cabinet because it never fills up completely. In fact, it actually *expands* to accommodate new knowledge. Thus as I explained earlier, the more you know about a field, the more you will be able to remember in that domain. In a similar vein, our memory system is significantly different from audio- or video-recorders. Whereas tapes record what actually happened, what we recall is not necessarily the same as what went into our minds originally. Research suggests that we store *interpretations* of events – not the actual experiences themselves. In other words, remembering is a *constructive* process in which we use prior knowledge and expectations to interpret what we *think* happened in the past. Therefore, many of our cherished memories are intriguing blends of fact and fiction. For example, although the famous psychologist Jean Piaget had a vivid memory of being kidnapped while being minded by his nanny, subsequent investigations revealed that she had fabricated the entire story in order to explain a clandestine meeting with a boy friend (Piaget, 1962). This means that Piaget must have unwittingly memorised a fictitious tale and 'experienced' it – even though it never happened. Finally, the way in which we search through our memory system differs from the way in which computers retrieve information. For example, if a computer were asked 'What is Shakespeare's telephone number?', it would search its memory files for entries under 'playwrights' and 'telephone numbers'. But when we are faced with the same question, we use our reasoning processes to decide not to waste any time in conducting a memory search to answer such a question. This example shows that our minds tend to work *faster* as we acquire more knowledge whereas computers slow down in similar circumstances. But if our minds do not work like computers when remembering things, then we should not expect to learn academic material in just one go. Instead, we should space our study sessions so that our learning is regular and brief (see pp. 34–6).

Stages of memory

What steps do we go through in our minds when we remember something? Psychologists have identified three stages of memory – encoding (or registration of information), storage (or retention) and retrieval (or looking up the desired material) (see Figure 1).

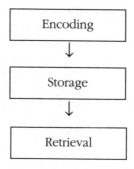

Fig. 1 Three Stages of Memory

The main task during the 'encoding stage' is to transform physical input from the senses into an abstract memory representation (e.g. words or images) that the brain can interpret. The next step in remembering (the 'storage stage') involves the maintenance or retention of this encoded information over time. Finally, in the 'retrieval stage', the stored information is consulted and brought into consciousness. Not surprisingly, if an error occurs at any of these three stages, forgetting can occur. Let us now examine each of these stages of memory in more detail.

Encoding

The term 'encoding' refers to the process by which we absorb information and convert it into a format (or code) that can be interpreted by the brain. Not surprisingly, different encoding strategies exist for the different information which we wish to remember. A visual code represents the information as a picture or a mental image. Alternatively, an acoustic code represents it as a sequence of sounds. Finally, a semantic code represents information in terms of its meaning to us. For example, when reading a chapter in a textbook, we should not try to remember all the words off by heart. Instead, we should endeavour to assess the general meaning or gist of the passage. If we do not encode information systematically, it will not leave any 'trace' in our minds. Accordingly, much of what we call forgetting originates from *inadequate encoding* of the material in the first place. If we are introduced to someone at a noisy party, is it any wonder that we fail to encode their name properly? In general, encoding problems are best tackled by investing more effort in one's studies (see 'overlearning' in Box 8.2).

Box 8.2 *Putting more effort into studying:*
The value of overlearning

Do you try to encode information in different ways when you study? Or are you so anxious to get it out of the way that you do not attend to it fully? Unfortunately, most students forget academic material because it never 'went in' properly in the first place. In general, there are two practical ways of overcoming this encoding problem. First, ask yourself 'What exactly do I want to learn in this study session?' before you open your books. If possible, give yourself 2–3 specific study questions for the session. Second, use the strategy of 'overlearning'. This technique involves consolidating what you have learned by going over it once more just to make sure that you understand it fully. In general, overlearning enhances encoding – especially if it is conducted repeatedly and in different contexts.

By the way, the most common reason for forgetting the names of people to whom you have been introduced recently is that you may not have paid sufficient attention to the information in the first place. A simple trick to overcome this type of encoding failure is to ask the person to spell his or her name for you. The double benefit here is that not only are you paying the person the compliment of wanting to get his/her name right but you are also receiving another chance to encode the details that you missed earlier.

The importance of encoding is recognised by 'levels of processing' theorists in memory research. These theorists believe that the durability of stored information depends on how 'deeply' it is encoded initially. Specifically, they suggest that information will decay quickly if it is processed only at a shallow level but will be memorised indefinitely if it is encoded more deeply. For example, imagine coming across a diagram in your textbook. In this situation, you could look at the colours in the picture (most superficial processing), read the labels attached to the diagram (deeper processing) or *try to find out what meaning or point the diagram is conveying* (deepest level of processing because it is concerned with the *meaning* of the information presented). In general, the last of these encoding strategies (looking for the *meaning* of the diagram) works best. This principle of depth of processing provides a logical foundation for the questioning part of the PQRR reading strategy (see also Chapter 5).

Storage

After information has been encoded, it has to be stored in memory in the form of words, pictures or motor actions. For example, a person's name (e.g. 'Marilyn') could be repeated as a series of three syllables ('Mar-i-lin') or it could be stored as a mental image (e.g. as a picture of Marilyn Monroe). But a skill such as driving a car cannot be represented verbally. Instead, it is stored most effectively as a motor 'programme' which is activated mainly through physical practice. Interestingly, most storage strategies depend on *repetition* of the information to be learned. This process is called 'maintenance rehearsal' and can be used when you come across the definition of a new term in a book. When this happens, you should pause and repeat this definition slowly to yourself. Unfortunately, storage failure among students occurs when they race through a difficult passage in a textbook – a flaw which, you may recall, characterises the reading habits of unsuccessful students (see Chapter 1, p. 8).

Retrieval

When you want to locate a book in the university library, you need to know its reference number. This identification code enables you to retrieve the book – assuming it has not been borrowed or mis-shelved. Similarly, it's no use having information in your head if you cannot *call it up* when you need it. In the retrieval stage of memory, therefore, our task is pick out what we need from permanent storage in our minds. To do this successfully, we need a retrieval cue (e.g. an acronym like ROYGBIV for the colours of the rainbow) to trigger the desired information. If we fail to prepare such cues when we study, we are likely to experience the frustration of the 'tip of the tongue phenomenon'. This all too familiar state of mind is characterised by the feeling that we *know* that we know the answer to a question but cannot retrieve it at that precise moment. Mysteriously, the elusive answer invariably pops into our minds at some later date – suggesting the existence of unconscious retrieval processes.

Interestingly, our retrieval processes seem to be remarkably context-dependent. In other words, we tend to encode features of the *environment* as well as the material which we set out to learn. For example, people tend to remember information better when their attempted recall takes place in a similar environment or context to the one in which the original learning occurred. To explain, the closer the resemblance between testing and learning conditions, the better is the recall. Consider an experiment in which deep-sea divers were asked to learn a list of unrelated words, either when they were on shore or under water. Later, their memories for these words were tested either in congruent conditions (in the same environment in which they had originally learned them) or in incongruent circumstances (in a different environment). Results showed that the divers recalled more words under the *congruent* rather than the incongruent circumstances (Sternberg, 1999). Intriguingly, the context-dependency of memory applies to *internal* as well as external environmental factors. Accordingly, a person's mental state (e.g. emotions) can affect his or her retrieval processes. Put simply, your physical or emotional condition may serve as a retrieval cue for what you have learned in a specific situation. For example, if you learn something when you are drunk, you will tend to recall it better when you are drunk than when you are sober! Based on this principle of state-dependency, the best way to guard against retrieval failure when studying is to test your memory for academic material as often as possible under exam-like conditions (see also Chapter 10).

In summary, research shows that memory performance is influenced by three main factors – the way in which the information is encoded initially, the manner in which it is stored and the type of cues that are present at retrieval. Therefore, the best way to improve your memory is to develop strategies which enhance each of these three processes. I shall return to this principle later in the chapter.

The structure of the memory system

People often complain about the frailty of their memories. They say 'I often forget people's names – my mind is like a sieve' as if memory were a unitary system. But research shows that memory comprises at least three separate stores (sensory, working and long-term memory), which have different functions and characteristics. Accordingly, it is common for people's memory for faces to be superior to their memory for names – a fact which is usually explained by encoding processes. Whereas faces can be encoded in two ways (as verbal labels and/or as pictures), names are usually coded only verbally.

The three main stores in the memory system are sensory memory (SM), short-term (more recently called 'working memory') memory (WM) and long-term memory (LTM). Before explaining these stores in detail, a short description of them may be helpful. To begin with, the information which reaches our eyes and ears is stored briefly in sensory registers which prolong a snapshot of this input until we decide whether or not to process it further. The purpose of this unconscious memory store is to keep a quick sensory impression of events which impinge upon us. Only a small proportion of the information that is registered in this manner is attended to and passed on to working memory where it is subjected to analysis. Here, the information is manipulated deliberately (e.g. through rehearsal) for a short while (about 15–30 seconds). With appropriate rehearsal, this information is then transferred from its temporary store to its final destination – long-term memory. Knowledge is retained according to its meaning in this store.

Forgetting involves different mechanisms in these three stores. For example, in the sensory registers, much of the registered information decays spontaneously before it is passed down the line to working memory. Forgetting from the short-term store, however, is usually caused by *interference* from distractors. If you hear a sudden noise while walking into a room, you may forget what you were looking for temporarily. Finally, forgetting in long-term memory is usually due to not having the right retrieval cue (e.g. when we experience the 'tip of the tongue phenomenon' described earlier).

Sensory memory

As I explained, information from the world is transmitted through the senses to the brain, where it is registered briefly without our awareness. The purpose of sensory memory (SM) is to prolong an exact image of each sensory experience for long enough to enable it to be processed further if required. Thus flashes of what you see and echoes of what you hear are held in your sensory registers for a split second before they decay. To illustrate this store, have you ever had the experience of asking someone to repeat a sentence that you were only half-listening to – only to discover that you 'heard' what they said before they actually repeated it? If so, then you have experienced auditory sensory memory (or echoic memory). Likewise, the persistence of visual information in your sensory register (called iconic memory) is responsible for your ability to see movement in films despite the fact that what you are looking at is actually a series of static images alternating with blank intervals. Iconic memory also accounts for the 'rubbery pencil effect' (demonstrated in Box 8.3).

Box 8.3 *The rubbery pencil effect*

Would you like to experience visual sensory memory? If so, try this exercise on the rubbery pencil effect. Take a pencil in your right hand. Grip it at the base between your thumb and forefinger (with the point at the top). Now, extend the arm out fully and slowly wave the pencil around. Notice how 'rubbery' it appears. This illusion is caused by the fact that your visual sensory memory system has created a time-lag between the actual and perceived position of the pencil in space. And your mind tries to make sense of this disparity by guessing that the pencil must be flexible or rubbery.

Unfortunately, information in sensory memory decays rapidly. Therefore, only a fraction of the information bombarding your senses is actually transferred to the next stage of the memory system – the short-term or working memory store.

Working memory

Working memory (WM) is a temporary but active store or receiving platform which holds a small amount of information while we are working on it (Logie, 1999). Just like a workbench, this store is designed to facilitate the conscious processing of information that is currently in use. Its capacity is limited and its duration is a matter of seconds rather than minutes. We can feel our working memories in action whenever we do some kind of deliberate mental activity. To illustrate, multiply 49 by 17 in your head. This task is difficult because it forces you both to store and to calculate numbers at the same time (7 by 9 is 63 – put down the 3 and carry the 6. Now, 7 by 4 is 28 . . .). Studies show that without deliberate rehearsal, information will be lost from your working memory in less than 30 seconds. To experience the characteristics of this store, try another task. Imagine standing in front of your house. How many windows can you see in your mind's eye? Now, count these windows to yourself. Here, your 'inner eye' (called the visuo-spatial scratchpad) allows you to inspect a visual image of your house and your 'inner voice' (called the articulatory loop) allows you to count each of the windows that you can 'see'.

Working memory is a fragile but invaluable system which is involved whenever you have to remember information for brief periods of time (e.g. when listening to sentences, looking up a phone number or when checking your change in a shop). As I explained, it is facilitated by deliberate repetition of the information to be remembered. But there are two different types of repetition: maintenance and 'elaborative rehearsal'. The former type, which consists of saying something over and over again to yourself, helps to keep information alive in short-term memory. But it does not guarantee the establishment of long-term memories. In fact, as soon as rote repetition stops, the information disappears. Another form of repetition is therefore needed to ensure the consolidation of our knowledge – or its safe transfer to a more permanent base in long-term memory. This brings us to elaborative rehearsal which involves *thinking about the meaning* of the new material and trying to relate it to what we already know. For example, what does a new term that we encounter remind us of? In general, elaborative rehearsal produces deeper encoding of material than does maintenance rehearsal and leads to better recall. Unfortunately, many students prefer to use maintenance rehearsal in situations where elaborative rehearsal is more appropriate.

Long-term memory

Long-term memory (LTM) contains everything which we know about the world. This store is an unconscious system for storing vast amounts of knowledge (names, dates, rules, skills) for indefinite durations which can range from a few minutes to an entire lifetime. This knowledge includes both factual information (general facts about the world as well as unique personal experiences) and procedural skills (e.g. how to tie your shoe laces). Within LTM, our knowledge is dynamically organised in meaningful units called schemas (which are mental representations of categories of people, objects and events; see Chapter 4). Evidence of this *semantic* organisation of long-term memory comes from the pattern of mistakes which people tend to make when recalling information from this store. For example, they might say 'ship' instead of 'boat' – indicating that they had stored the word according to its *meaning* rather than its sound.

Since LTM is organised semantically, then the way in which we impose meaning on or *interpret* the past is critical to the way in which we recall it. In short, we recall what we *think* happened – not necessarily what actually occurred (see also p. 103).

Practical techniques to improve your understanding and memory

The popularity of cue cards, shopping lists, pocket diaries, desk calendars and electronic organisers indicates the importance which we attach to remembering things. Unfortunately, although these external memory aids can enhance your ability to recall certain kinds of information (e.g. isolated facts), they do not increase your *understanding* of this material. Therefore, you need some practical techniques to improve the efficiency of your encoding, storage and retrieval processes. In this regard, the most useful memory techniques are those which *impose organisation* on what you have to learn and which encourage you to *relate* this material to *what you already know*. In short, the more effort you invest in understanding something, the better you will remember it. But what exactly is 'understanding'?

The term understanding refers to our ability to interpret, explain or impose meaning on things. It is *built up* from the way in which we use our background knowledge and assumptions to draw conclusions about what we hear or see. For example, consider how we construct an understanding of the following sentence derived from a story called *The Wall* by Jean-Paul Sartre (see Norman, 1982).

> They pushed us into a large white room and my
> eyes began to blink because the light hurt them

What does this sentence suggest? Taken literally, the text describes an incident in which the narrator and others were pushed into a large white room. But notice how you use your knowledge and imagination to *go beyond* what you are told explicitly. For example, the fact that the narrator's eyes blinked suggests that s/he had been in a darkened room earlier. Furthermore, the word 'pushed' implies that s/he had left this room involuntarily. And the large white room might conjure up the image of a prison or a hospital. Clearly, our 'understanding' of such stories depends on our ability to 'fill in' the gaps in what we are told by using our knowledge and imagination constructively. But how can we do this in practice?

Improving your understanding

Psychologists have identified at least five techniques which improve our understanding of what we wish to learn. These techniques may be explained as follows.

Ask questions: Use the PQRR technique

According to the depth of processing principle (see section on encoding, pp. 104–6), *asking questions* about the *meaning* of the material that you are about to learn produces better understanding and subsequent recall than does passive reading of it. Therefore, develop the habit of using the PQRR strategy every time you read a book or set of notes (see Chapter 5 for more details). Asking questions improves storage processes in memory.

Pay more attention to what you have to learn

Since most forgetting is caused by inadequate initial encoding, you should make a special effort *to pay as much attention as possible* to the layout of the material you would like to learn. For example, write down the main headings in a chapter on a sheet of paper. This will highlight the material so that it can be absorbed easily.

Use headings (schemas) to organise the material

Based on the principle that organisation improves memory and understanding, you should look for or make up topic headings that describe the material which you wish to learn. To illustrate, do you

The more questions you ask about something, the more likely you are to remember it

think that you could remember the following passage (derived from an experiment by Dooling & Lachman, 1971)?

> Selling his jewels, the explorer ignored his rivals' taunts and sneers: 'I'll prove you wrong', he thundered, 'The earth is an egg not a table'. Surging through the watery expanse, the days became weeks and rumours grew that he had fallen off the edge. But at last, winged harbingers appeared and circled the explorers, indicating that the quest was over

Probably not – because this information lacks a frame of reference. But notice what happens when you are told that the passage is entitled 'Columbus Discovers America'. Armed with this heading, you can activate existing knowledge about Columbus (your Columbus schema) which gives you sufficient background knowledge to decode the meaning of the text. I made a similar point in Chapter 4 using the passage on washing clothes (p. 50). These examples illustrate the fact that headings enable you to organise what you are about to learn and activate any prior knowledge which you have about the topic in question. Based on this principle, you should always look for headings to describe the material that you are learning. Headings enhance all three steps in remembering – encoding, storage and retrieval.

Establish links with what you already know
As understanding depends on linking your ideas together, you should try to ask yourself 'what does this remind me of?' whenever you come across a new concept in your subject. Next, try to summarise 2–3 main ideas or learning points from the material in question. Finally, try to elaborate your summary by linking it with what you already know. These tips are based on the principle of elaborative rehearsal (see p. 110) which applies to storage and retrieval processes in memory.

Check what you have learned
Recent research shows that people's understanding of what they have read improves significantly when they check what they have learned. This activity is called 'comprehension monitoring' (Sternberg, 1999) and it enriches our storage and retrieval processes. It involves asking yourself such questions as: Do I understand the main idea in this passage? Does it make sense to me? And can I explain it in my own words?

A summary of these aids to understanding is presented in Box 8.4 together with the principles on which they are based.

Box 8.4   *Techniques for improving understanding*

1. *Write down 2–3 specific questions about the material to be learned before you read it (depth of processing)*

2. *Make a special effort to pay attention to the layout of the material when you read it first (enhanced encoding)*

3. *Use headings to organise the material (schematic processing)*

4. *Establish links with what you already know (elaborative rehearsal)*

5. *Check what you have learned after every study session (comprehension monitoring)*

Strategies to improve rote learning

In the previous section, I explained how to increase your ability to make sense of things – to achieve *conceptual* understanding. But occasionally, you will have to learn things off by heart because they provide the building blocks for mastery of other material. For example, what are the names of the cranial nerves? Or what are the main parts of the ear? In both cases, some degree of rote-learning is required. For this purpose, mnemonics (psychological techniques for remembering things) based on rhymes and acronyms are especially useful. To illustrate, a rhyme like 'On Old Olympia's Towering Top A Finn And German Vault and Hop' may help you to remember the names of the cranial nerves (namely, olfactory, optic, oculomotor, trochlear, trigeminal, abducens, facial, auditory, glossopharyngeal, vagus and hypoglossal). Similarly, the acronym PET can be used to recall the names of the different parts of the ear – namely, pinna, ear canal and tympanic membrane.

In Box 8.5, I present a list of mnemonics which can facilitate rote-learning.

One of the most popular mnemonics listed in this box is the 'linkword' method (see Gruneberg, 1985) for teaching a vocabulary in a foreign language. To illustrate its use, let us consider a study by Raugh & Atkinson (1975). These researchers compared two ways of

| Box 8.5 | *Techniques for improving rote learning* |

Mnemonic	Example
1. Pegwords and imagery *(Imagine each item to be remembered as being 'stuck' in the object listed in the following rhyme)*	*One is a bun* *Two is a shoe* *Three is a tree* *Four is a door* *Five is a hive* *Six is sticks* *Seven is heaven* *Eight is a gate* *Nine is a mine* *Ten is a hen*
2. Linkwords *(Try to form a link between a new word or term in a foreign language and a familiar one)*	*e.g. nappe is the French word for tablecloth – so imagine taking a 'nap' on a tablecloth*
3. Acrostics *(Devise a sentence in which the first letters of the words represent the item to be remembered)*	*Every Good Boy Deserves Favour (E, G, B, D, F) To remember the names of the notes on the treble clef in music*
4. Acronyms *(Devise a word whose letters stand for the items to be remembered)*	*PQRR reading technique (Preview, question read and review)*

learning Spanish words. The first method involved traditional rote learning or trying to memorise off by heart English translations of the Spanish words. The second technique involved the linkword method whereby students were taught to *add meaning* to their learning in two stages. First, they were encouraged to think of an English word that sounded like the Spanish word in question (e.g. charcoal for the Spanish word *charco*, meaning 'puddle'). This English word served as a linkword. Then, they had to form an *interactive mental image* of this linkword embedded in its actual English translation. In this case, some charcoal could be imagined lying in a puddle. Results showed that students using the linkword method recalled an average of 88 per cent of the Spanish vocabulary words whereas the rote-learning group could recall only 28 per cent of these words. The implication of this study is that imagery-based procedures like linkwords could help you to remember new words in a foreign language.

Before we conclude this section, it is important to explain why the mnemonics listed in Box 8.4 and Box 8.5 help to improve memory. Briefly, they work by strengthening each of the three stages of memory I outlined earlier in this chapter. First, they encourage us to pay extra attention to the material to be learned, thereby enhancing the encoding process. Second, mnemonics help us to organise or 'chunk' the material meaningfully. Third, they improve the retrieval process by training the learner to associate new information with familiar cues. For example, in the pegword method, the items to be learned are linked with a set of mental pegs that already exist in memory. But the paradox of mnemonics is that they do not *simplify* what we have to learn – instead, they elaborate upon it. Therefore, they allow us to store *more* rather than less knowledge about the material in question (Bernstein *et al.*, 2000). And this brings us right back to the principle from which we started. Knowledge is power – the more you know, the more you can remember. To remind you of what you learned in this chapter, a list of key memory principles is provided in the Appendix (see pp. 117–18).

Summary

The purpose of this chapter was to explore what memory is and to provide some practical techniques to improve your ability to understand and remember what you learn in university. I began by explaining that human memory differs from other storage devices because it *expands* to accommodate new information. Therefore, *understanding* is the key to effective memory. Put simply, the more you know and understand, the more you can remember. But to remember anything, three steps are required. First, you must register or encode the information properly. Second, you must store this knowledge in some format (e.g. as a mental image) that the mind can understand. Finally, you have to be able to retrieve it when necessary. If you fail to perform any of these three stages correctly, forgetting can occur. For example, daydreaming at a lecture leads to encoding failure whereas a failure to check regularly what you know can cause retrieval failure. We then learned that the memory system comprises three main stores: sensory, short-term (working), and long-term memory. The characteristics of each of these stores were outlined briefly. In the next section, I reviewed five psychological techniques which can improve your understanding and memory. These techniques consisted of asking questions (using the PQRR approach; see Chapter 5), paying more attention to the material to be learned, using headings (or schemas) to organise this information, establishing links between what you have to learn and what you already know and checking what you have learned at the end of every study session. The final section of the chapter considered some mnemonics designed for situations in which rote learning is required. These mnemonics consisted of pegwords, linkwords, acrostics and acronyms. The main principle underlying this chapter was the idea that your memory will improve when you make an effort to *organise* what you have to learn and to *relate it* to *what you already know.*

Answer to memory puzzle in Box 8.1 (p. 102)

The 24 digits are generated by the rule 'squaring numbers from 1 to 12'. Thus the square of 1 is 1, and that of 2 is 4 and so on, until the last number, 144, which is the square of 12.

Appendix to Chapter 8. Some Principles of Remembering and Understanding

Here is a summary of the main principles of understanding and memory that were explained in this chapter.

Organisation (chunking)
Organising individual items into meaningful groups (or chunks) helps to improve the span of your short-term memory.

Constructive nature of memory
Remembering is a constructive process in which we use prior knowledge and expectations to interpret what we *think* happened in the past.

Overlearning
Our memory can be improved by developing the habit of reviewing what we learned at the end of a study session – even if we feel sure that we have mastered the material adequately.

Depth of processing

The durability of our memories is determined, in part, by the *depth* of questioning (or level of processing) which we conducted on the material initially.

Maintenance rehearsal

Information can be kept alive in our short-term or working memory as long as it is rehearsed or repeated to ourselves.

Elaborative rehearsal

For information to be stored permanently in our memory, we need to make an effort to link it meaningfully to what we already know.

Advance organisers: The importance of schemas

Looking for an appropriate heading or schema at the encoding stage improves understanding and memory of the material to be learned.

Knowledge-base effect

The more one knows about some field (i.e. the larger one's 'knowledge-base'), the better one's memory will be for new information that is relevant to this area.

Encoding-specificity principle of memory

The probability of remembering information is improved if the conditions at retrieval resemble as closely as possible the conditions under which the original learning occurred. In other words, the closer the match between the conditions present at encoding and those at retrieval, the better will be the memory performance. This principle applies both to physical (the 'context-dependency' of learning) and to psychological (the 'state-dependency' of learning) environments.

9. Planning and Writing Essays, Papers and Research Projects

'How can I tell what I think till I see what I say?' (E. M. Forster, 1927)

'The last thing one finds out when constructing a work is what to put first'
(Blaise Pascal, 1670)

Introduction

The ability to marshal relevant evidence and to express one's ideas clearly in writing has long been admired as a distinctive characteristic of the educated mind. Therefore, no matter what subject you are studying in university, you will be expected to write various research assignments (e.g. essays, term papers, seminar presentations, book reviews, case studies, laboratory reports and project dissertations) in partial fulfilment of the requirements of your academic course. The purpose of these assignments is three-fold. First, they assess the degree to which you can apply general academic knowledge to specific problems. Second, they train you to master certain writing conventions (e.g. how to cite references properly) in your subject. Finally, as the novelist E.M. Forster observed, writing assignments help you to clarify and externalise your thinking about a given topic. To explain, you may not discover what you really believe about something until you have to write about it. Accordingly, writing an essay allows us to inform *ourselves* as well as our readers. Given this background, the purpose of the present chapter is to provide some practical advice on planning, researching and writing academic assignments (see also Blaxter *et al.*, 1996; Northedge, 1990; Race, 2000).

To begin with, I shall consider the problem of planning your assignment. Next, I shall present some practical guidelines on researching it as thoroughly as possible. Then, I shall explore some strategies for writing a first draft of your work. As we shall see, this draft is written mainly for yourself – to clarify your thinking. Finally, on the basis that all good writing involves *rewriting*, I shall explain how to prepare a final version of your work. A diagram of the stages involved in conducting research is presented overleaf (see Figure 1).

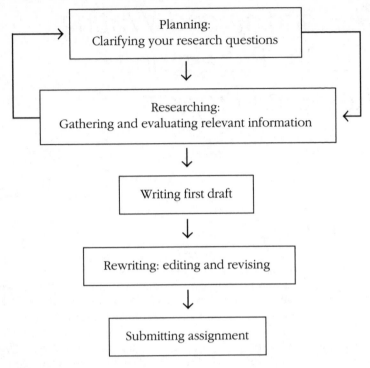

Fig. 1 The Main Stages of Research

Planning your assignment

Research is difficult for many students because nobody tells you *how* to start or *when* to stop writing. To overcome the 'start up' problem, you need to perform three main tasks: clarifying the assignment, choosing your topic and specifying your research question(s).

Clarifying the assignment

The first step in conducting a research assignment is find out exactly what is expected of you academically. For this task, do not rely on second hand information conveyed to you by other students because it may be incomplete or inaccurate. The best way to establish the parameters of your assignment is to ask questions of the academic staff concerned (see Box 9.1 opposite). Never make assumptions about your assignment – check relevant details with your Department. If possible, try to locate and read any written guidelines which you may have been given about the assignment. Looking at a copy of a

---

| **Box 9.1** | *Clarifying your assignment:* |
| | *Some questions to ask your Department* |

Here are some questions to ask the academic staff who are responsible for the assignment which you have to undertake.

If an academic supervisor is required, how will you obtain, or be assigned to, one?

Can you obtain a copy of any written regulations that apply to your research assignment?

What is expected of you in this project (e.g. in terms of the structure, content and originality of the material)?

What is the deadline for submission of the assignment?

What is the maximum word length allowed?

What system of stylistic conventions (e.g. margin, spacing, reference citations, footnotes) is required for your assignment?

Is it possible to inspect a good example of the type of assignment that is required of you?

---

previous assignment from another year may also help you to develop a mental model of what you will have to produce.

Choosing your topic

The next step in the initial phase of research is to choose your research topic. Ideally, this topic should satisfy at least three criteria. Specifically, it should be appropriate, feasible and appealing to you – but not necessarily original (because at undergraduate level, one is still 'learning the ropes').

The criterion of appropriateness is satisfied if your topic is approved formally by your academic department. Of course, this problem does not arise if the topic has been *assigned* to you but it could become an issue if you have to devise the topic yourself. In this latter case, it is helpful to consult staff members for possible project ideas. The advantage of this approach is that it ensures that your supervisor will be interested in your work. Other strategies for generating possible research topics are listed in Box 9.2 overleaf.

The second criterion for a suitable research topic is that it should be feasible or manageable within the time-limit and resources available

Box 9.2 *Generating ideas for possible research topics*

According to Blaxter *et al.* (1996), there are a number of practical tips which can help you to generate suitable research questions. In each case, however, you must seek formal approval of your idea from your academic supervisor.

Ask a staff member for ideas which s/he is currently working on so that your project may be of assistance to him/her

Look at previous projects by students and try to modify or extend one of them

Find an exam question from a previous year and try to re-formulate it as a research question for your project

Keep an 'idea file' of puzzles and paradoxes that you come across in your reading

Skim through the contents pages of a major journal in your field – paying special attention to the suggestions for further research in the section at the end

to you. For example, it would be inadvisable to undertake an assignment on a topic which is not covered by your university library. In general, the most feasible research topics are those which have generated sufficient research literature to whet your appetite but not so much as to overwhelm you with technical detail.

Thirdly, the topic for your assignment should hold some interest for you as you will be studying it for some time. But what makes a topic interesting? Remember from Chapter 6 that interest is a 'two way street'. In other words, it is as much an *investment* in something as a return from it. So, don't wait for something to interest you – take the initiative by asking as many questions as possible about it. The clearer and more specific your questions, the more they will captivate your interest.

Specifying your research question(s)

The next stage in the research process is to specify the question(s) which you wish to answer as precisely as possible. But remember that *statements* are not questions. If your friend tells you that she is studying early twentieth-century Irish poets, then you have a *description* of her topic. But if she says 'I'm trying to find out what influence the 1916 Rising had on the themes of Irish poets in the 1920s', then you can identify her research question and become more involved in her work. This example shows that statements generate less interest than do questions. Not surprisingly, successful researchers understand this difference between a topic and a question. Whereas a topic may refer to a general academic field (e.g. law of contract), a research question is a specific problem within that area (e.g. 'What constitutes "economic duress" in contract?'). A list of sample research questions is presented in Box 5.3, Chapter 5 (p. 62).

When you have specified your research question as precisely as possible, it is essential to calculate how much time you will have for your project (see also Chapter 3). A useful tip here is to work backwards from the date of submission to the present time. But remember, a cardinal rule of research is that *everything takes longer* than you expect! To counteract this problem, and to apply the SMART approach described in Chaper 2, you should give yourself a specific starting and finishing time for each step of your proposed research plan.

Researching your assignment: Gathering and evaluating relevant information

The next major stage of research is to gather and evaluate relevant information. This data gathering work involves at least four key tasks: locating relevant background literature, evaluating such information, taking relevant notes and documenting your reference sources correctly.

Background research: Locating and reading relevant literature

The amount of background research which you conduct for your assignment will depend on such factors as the nature and length of your assignment (e.g. is it a weekly legal case-study or a year-long dissertation?), its importance (i.e. what proportion of end-of-year marks does it count for?) and the subject matter involved (e.g. whether it is library- or laboratory-based). Assuming that some library work is necessary, you should learn how to use such research facilities as internet search engines (e.g. Google, Alta Vista), on-line retrieval catalogues (which enable you to search for books and periodicals by title, name and keyword) and specialist reference sources on CD-ROM machines (e.g. Med Line, Psyc Lit) in your subject. Make sure that you know where such facilities are located in your library. You should also find out how to use your inter-library loan facility as you may wish to borrow articles and/or books from other libraries. But do not delay your assignment until such material arrives as this information may not be what you had expected. Above all, try not to become side-tracked by irrelevant literature at this stage. The only way to avoid this pitfall is to keep a *written statement* of your research question at hand when you start your literature search. This statement should contain key words which will guide your search.

At this stage, a quick scan of relevant research literature may be helpful. The purpose of this search is to find out what other investigators have written about the question in which you are interested. A consultation with academic staff members or reference librarians in your subject could help you to get started. Leaflets are normally available in your library to explain the nature and location of special bibliographical sources such as the *Social Sciences Citation Index* or the *Science Citation Index*.

Evaluating relevant literature

Locating relevant research literature only tells you what other people have done. It does not tell you how *valid* this information is or what to do next. Therefore, the next stage of research is to conduct a literature review or critical evaluation of relevant information. A checklist of practical guidelines for this purpose are provided in Chapter 7 (see pp. 98–9).

Taking notes

As you use your critical reading checklist, try to take summary notes. But make sure to check from time to time that these notes are relevant to your specific research question(s) (see advice on note-taking in Chapter 5, p. 68). Otherwise, you may end up with a series of unrelated facts from different studies. And there is nothing more dreary than an essay or report which comprises a funeral-parade of unrelated facts. If possible, read primary literature sources rather than textbooks in order to minimise errors of distortion and other misconceptions (Shermer, 1997).

Documenting your reference sources

Develop the habit of recording the complete publication details of any reference sources (e.g. books and articles) that you intend to use in your assignment. You can do this in one of two ways – by hand or by computer. First, you could write key reference details (e.g. author, title, year of publication, city of publication and publisher) on index cards. The advantage of this approach is that such cards are light, portable and amenable to alphabetical organisation. Alternatively, a number of automated bibliographical databases (or reference managers) are now available commercially. The advantage of these systems is that they can be searched rapidly and printed out in a format that is appropriate to your discipline.

Regardless of the approach that you use, be careful to record the exact page numbers of any important ideas or quotations. Unless you do this, you may be guilty of using other people's material as your own – a serious offence which is called plagiarism. This term refers to a form of intellectual theft which involves copying other people's writing, work or ideas and subsequently passing them off as one's own material.

Getting your ideas down on paper: Writing the first draft of your assignment

Having located and evaluated relevant literature, you should now begin to write a first draft of your assignment. As I explained previously, the objective of this draft is to clarify your own thinking about the project. Transmitting this information clearly to the reader is the task facing you in the next draft. Before you begin, however, you should understand the following points.

First, your writing must be clear and coherent. This requirement stems from the fact that unless you will be examined orally, your reader will not be able to question you directly about what you have written. So make sure that you do not end up contributing unwittingly to the 'gems of wisdom' in Box 9.3.

Second, unless you are very lucky or extremely gifted, you will not be able to write an adequate essay or report in one sitting. Therefore, all you should concern yourself with at this stage is to get your ideas down on paper in any order. You can reorganise them later. And that is why, to paraphrase Nabokov (see Chapter 5), good writing depends on substantial *rewriting* or the art of refining your ideas progressively. Third, when you write, you must be punctilious about citing appropriate reference sources for any ideas or quotations which you borrowed from other authors. Otherwise, you may be charged with plagiarism. Finally, you should realise that considerable effort is required to write an assignment clearly and with an appealing flow. In other words, good writing depends more on perspiration than

---

Box 9.3	Ambiguity: Some gems of wisdom

Sometimes, what we write may not reflect what we had intended to say. The following examples of ambiguity and malapropisms have been gathered from examination answers and from written assignments. Make sure that you don't add material to this list!

'Girls grow up to be women quicker than boys do'

'As regards sex, I wouldn't go all the way with Freud'

'The subjects were both male and female'

'The Ss consisted of 21 students from UCD with an equal distribution of both genders'

'Europeans speak from left to right whereas Arabs speak from right to left'

'The Pyramids are a range of mountains between France and Spain'

'Louis Pasteur discovered a cure for rabbis'

'Involuntary muscles are not as willing as voluntary muscles'

'As the rain forests in the Amazon are shrinking, so too are the Indians'

---

on inspiration (see Peter de Vries's remark on p. 14). But what makes a piece of expository writing successful?

According to Northedge (1990), there are at least three distinctive features of a successful piece of expository writing.

• *It answers the question asked*

All too often, students re-interpret an essay title in their minds to mean 'Write whatever comes to mind about X'. By taking this approach, you are ignoring the specific question or issue raised by the title of the essay and are in danger of going off on a tangent of irrelevance.

• *It draws on relevant course material*

Most written assignments in university require you to look up relevant course material before you answer the specific question under investigation. Therefore, writing offers you an opportunity to use relevant course work as evidence to support what you wish to say.

• *It presents a coherent argument or approach*

The evidence and arguments in a well-written assignment seem to hang together coherently. There are three main strategies for achieving this coherence: (i) proper planning and clear structural organisation (e.g. allocating a separate paragraph for each main idea); (ii) the use of 'signpost words' (such as, 'therefore', 'so') and (iii) the discipline of engaging in successive revisions of your work.

Making a preliminary outline of your essay or report

Before you begin to write, it is essential to make a 'map' or outline of the sequence of your ideas. This outline should address such issues as the specific research question(s) that you wish to tackle, the scope and limitations of your assignment and the evidence and arguments that you wish to use in your writing. If you find it difficult to specify your research questions clearly, then you need to go back to the drawing board and analyse the topic of the assignment once more.

In general, a good outline should examine both the *content* and *structure* of your assignment. With regard to content, what is the main conclusion, point or argument that you wish to present? What would you like readers to *believe* or to *do* after they have read your work? What evidence, arguments or examples can you use to support your position? Turning to *structural* issues, you should ask yourself the following questions. What are main ideas which serve as a foundation for your 'building' (i.e. your assignment)? What is the optimum sequence in which to present these ideas so that they flow logically? Unless your assignment has a pre-determined format (e.g. as found in laboratory reports in psychology), you will have to design the scaffolding or structure of your work on your own. In this regard, it may help to divide the assignment into three parts: beginning (introduction), middle (main body) and end (conclusions and implications). The purpose of the introduction is to explain the background to your research question(s). The main body of the report conveys details of relevant evidence and arguments. Finally, the conclusion draws together your argument or findings in a concise manner. Please note, however, that the introduction, main body and conclusions of your assignment do *not* have to be written in the sequence in which they are presented. As Strunk & White (1979) pointed out, 'writing, to be effective, must follow closely the thoughts of the writer, but not necessarily in the order in which these thoughts occur' (p. 15).

Having made an outline of your paper, you should now rearrange your notes in the appropriate sequence. Then give yourself an uninterrupted period of time (usually not less than one and a half hours) and start writing. As this is the first draft, your main objective at this stage should be to get all your ideas down on paper. Once the essential details are in place, you can revise the paper at your leisure.

Organising your material

Having sketched an outline of the content and structure of your assignment, the next task is impose some kind of organisation on your ideas. In effect, this means that you have to decide which points and which lines of evidence 'hang together' best. Put to one side any material that seems irrelevant to your argument.

In general, each of your key points should be given a separate paragraph. Furthermore, Strunk & White (1979) recommend that you should begin each paragraph either with a topic sentence (a general statement about the issue being discussed in that section of the essay or report) or with a transition word or phrase (see Box 9.4, p. 132, for some examples). The remaining sentences in the paragraph should explain, expand, illustrate or modify this central point. As Winston Churchill observed, 'Just as the sentence contains one idea in all its fullness, so the paragraph should embrace a distinct episode; and as sentences should follow one another in harmonious sequence, so paragraphs must fit into one another like the automatic couplings of railway carriages' (cited in Marshall & Rowland, 1993, pp. 173–4). Usually, it is best to present the topic sentence first so that the reader will have some idea of what to expect in the paragraph. In other words, the first sentence of every paragraph should act as an 'advance organiser' for the remaining material in it.

Writing the introduction to the assignment

The purpose of the introduction is to set the scene for your assignment. As a first step in this task, you need to specify the *scope* and *limitations* of your work. By outlining what you intend to cover (i.e. the scope of your assignment) and by indicating what you intend to omit (i.e. the limitations of the work), you are indicating the criteria by which you wish your assignment will be assessed. In a sense, therefore, you can influence the criteria by which your assignment will be judged.

Experienced researchers tend to write the introduction last. Recall what the French philosopher Pascal said about this strategy at the beginning of this chapter (see p. 119). This advice may surprise you but there are several reasons for this strategy. First, it will give your writing an attractive flow because by knowing what your conclusions are, you can introduce enough background material to ensure that there is a visible narrative thread linking the material together. Second, leaving the introduction until the end reduces the likelihood of including *irrelevant* material in the introduction. Finally, when you know what your conclusions are, you are in a good position to devise an imaginative or engaging *opening* to your work. This is particularly relevant to Arts subjects like English or history where a paper should present a *theme* rather than a mere summary of unrelated facts or other people's opinions. For example, you could start an essay on Oscar Wilde by arguing that he joked only about serious issues. Remember, the golden rule is to provide the reader with only enough information to enable him or her to understand the background to, and significance of, your specific question. Don't include excessive or irrelevant historical details.

Working on the main body of the text

Start with the middle part or main body of the assignment. Your main task here is to ensure that you cover what you said you would include (see your 'scope and limitations' section). The key issue at this stage is whether or not you have made sufficient points to support your conclusions. Remember that you must substantiate all your claims with appropriate evidence. Therefore, you must learn the art of referring to, or quoting from, scholarly sources in an effort to buttress your argument or exposition. Do not worry if the structure of your report changes as you make progress in writing the main body of the paper. It is quite common for writers to discover that the expression of one idea triggers another idea which challenges the way in which the introduction will have to be written.

Identifying and explaining your conclusions

The final section of your assignment is usually devoted to the conclusions. Here, your task is to indicate what follows from what – or to state explicitly the conclusions which are warranted by the evidence or arguments which you used. Ideally, your conclusions should be numbered or organised in such a way as to provide a general answer to your initial research question. As well as being cautious about premature extrapolation from your conclusions, you should outline some specific suggestions for future research on the topic you have addressed.

Writing a summary of your work

Most written assignments require an 'abstract', or brief summary of your work (usually amounting to no more than 200 words), to be included on a separate page. This abstract should be presented immediately after the title page and before the introduction. The purpose of the abstract is to explain concisely what research question you tackled, what evidence or arguments you presented and what conclusions you drew.

A note on the format and presentation of your work

The publication conventions surrounding academic assignments (e.g. how to cite and present references) vary from subject to subject. You must therefore familiarise yourself thoroughly with the writing conventions that are appropriate to your discipline. This information should be available from academic staff.

Preparing the final draft of your assignment: Tips on rewriting

Earlier, I said that successful writing depends on a progressive refinement of preliminary drafts. In other words, all writing involves rewriting. But how can you get from a disjointed initial draft to a polished and persuasive final version?

The first step in this process of revision involves reading your first draft from start to finish. Then read this draft again – but this time, more slowly and more critically. Make annotations and amendments to the text as you go along. More precisely, you should pay attention to at least three issues.

Coverage: Did you fulfil your stated objectives?

An important criterion to use when evaluating your first draft concerns the issue of whether or not you covered adequately everything that you said you would include. In other words, does the *content* reflect your *intent* (as stated in the scope and limitations part of your introduction)? When this question is posed, most people discover that some of their best points are not explained clearly enough or are missing. Although this discovery is disappointing, it is better for you to discover the gaps in your work at this stage than at a later date. By the way, you may find it helpful to ask a second reader (e.g. one of your lecturers or classmates) to comment briefly on the content and layout of your assignment.

Coherence: Do your ideas hang together?

The next criterion of effective writing concerns the coherence of the assignment. Do your ideas fit together neatly or do they appear to be rather random and disjointed? If there is neither a coherence nor a flow to your ideas, then you should consider using one or more of the following techniques. First, check that your headings and sub-headings are accurate and in the correct place. If the organisation of the paper is unclear or idiosyncratic, then the reader will not know what to expect next – and his or her surprise will soon turn to exasperation. Second, you should develop a skill in using 'transition words' to achieve a seamless connection between your paragraphs. These words provide the cement between the building blocks of your ideas. Some of them are listed in Box 9.4 overleaf.

Finally, for optimal flow in a paper, try to ensure that your conclusions are clearly apparent to the reader. A good way to do this is to write in your introduction: 'In this paper, I shall argue that . . .'. If your conclusions cannot be found easily, your work will appear to be confusing and incomplete.

Presentation: Does your paper have a professional appearance?

All things being equal, the more professional the appearance of your assignment, the more marks it will attract. Therefore, when checking your first draft, you should assess the clarity, grammar and style of your work. Let us address each of these issues in turn.

The clarity of an assignment can be assessed only with the assistance of a another reader. For example, you could ask a classmate or a friend to check that s/he understands what you have written (a favour which you can reciprocate when his or her project is being composed). This second reading is helpful because writers tend to become so familiar with their own work that they find it difficult to assess it objectively. Next, you should check that your spelling and grammar are satisfactory. Given the ubiquity of computerised spelling checkers, there is no excuse for errors in this aspect of your work. Also, you should use the active rather than the passive voice whenever possible. This advice is based on the theory that statements written in the passive voice tend to be duller and more difficult to read than those expressed in the active voice. For example, 'Michael Collins said that . . .' is more vibrant than is 'It was once said by Michael Collins that . . .'. Finally, you should check that you have complied fully with the stylistic conventions of your assignment. For

---

Box 9.4 *Some useful transition words and phrases*

One of the key skills of effective writing is to ensure that ideas flow smoothly between paragraphs. This fluency is best achieved by using transition words. These words are linking devices or linguistic signposts which provide good clues to the organisation of the material as well as indicating that something important is about to be presented. Here are some examples (from Deem, 1993; Marshall & Rowland, 1993):

Transition word/phrase	Function in writing
For example, for instance, to illustrate	to signal examples
Further, furthermore, in addition, also, in addition, moreover, next	to provide extra information
Likewise, similarly, also	to indicate a comparison
But, nevertheless, in contrast, on the other hand, conversely	to indicate a contrast
Therefore, overall, accordingly, so, consequently, thus	to indicate a cause-and-effect or a result/conclusion
First, second, third, finally, later, next, in the meantime, meanwhile	to indicate a chronological organisation/connection in time
In conclusion, to conclude, in other words, in short, on the whole	to provide a summary

---

example, when citing references is it conventional to use numbers and endnotes or to include in the text the author's surname and year of publication. Although these conventions vary considerably from subject to subject, it is your responsibility to learn the stylistic requirements of your subject. Although footnotes are commonly used in the Arts and Humanities (e.g. Philosophy and English), they are quite rare in the Social Sciences. In view of such stylistic variation, make sure to check a publication manual in your subject or else request written guidelines from your department before you begin your final draft. Avoid the use of sexist language also. Finally, some ironic guidelines on effective writing are presented (tongue in cheek) in Box 9.5.

Box 9.5   *Ironic rules of good writing*

1. *Alliteration always alienates.*

2. *Avoid clichés like the plague as they are the thin edge of the wedge.*

3. *It is wrong to ever split an infinitive in your sentences.*

4. *Using analogies in writing is like making chalk marks on water.*

5. *Why bother to include rhetorical questions in your work?*

6. *The passive voice is to be avoided in your work.*

Reviewing the final draft

Having re-written your assignment, you should review it once more using the following checklist:

(i)   What is your research question?

(ii)   Are you sure that you have addressed all of the key words in the title of the assignment?

(iii)   Did you cover what you said that you would cover?

(iv)   Does the paper/essay satisfy all relevant academic departmental regulations (e.g. with regard to format, word length)?

(v)   Does your work have a clear beginning and end? Is the layout and paragraph structure acceptable?

(vi)   Are all tables, graphs and other figures readily comprehensible and clearly labelled?

(vii) Have you listed precise references for each name that you cite in the your assignment? If so, are your references accurate and presented correctly?

(viii) Does the paper flow smoothly? If not, try inserting transition words and phrases at the junctions between paragraphs (see Box 9.4, p. 132).

Submitting the final draft

When you are happy with the final draft of the assignment, you should proof-read what you have written very carefully. It is not sufficient to use automated spelling checkers because they will not detect errors involving the inclusion or omission of correctly spelled but inappropriate words (e.g. 'form' rather than 'from'). Next, make sure to copy your final document several times before submitting it. Otherwise, you could lose the only copy of your work. Print out the assignment at least two days before the submission deadline to avoid any last-minute problems with computers. Try to obtain a receipt from your department when you submit the assignment formally. Do not resort to shoving your completed assignment under the door of a staff member on the evening of the deadline!

Responding to feedback on your assignment

Earlier in the chapter, I explained that writing is best regarded as a cycle of planning, drafting, revising, engaging in more planning, writing again and revising various drafts of your material in accordance with the demands of the assignment. You might think that this cycle culminates in the submission of your work. But this idea is wrong – because to be a successful researcher, you must participate in another step in the research process. This step involves using feedback on, and constructive criticism of, your work to improve the quality of your next assignment. In this regard, the following suggestions are intended to provide some practical tips on seeking and using helpful comments from academic staff.

- Do not take the marker's comments personally. There is a big difference between the 'real you' and the '*role* you'. So try to accept what your supervisor says as feedback designed to help your performance in future

- Ask for specific suggestions about how your work can be improved. These suggestions could be broken down by each major section of the paper (e.g. introduction, main body, conclusions)

• If your mark is disappointing, ask the corrector if s/he would mind reading a preliminary draft of your next assignment so that you can incorporate his/her advice before submitting the final draft the next time

Summary

The ability to adduce relevant evidence in support of clear and concise written arguments has long been valued in university education. Therefore, no matter what subject you are studying, you will be expected to master the art of planning, researching and writing up various kinds of academic assignments (e.g. essays, term papers and project dissertations). This chapter attempted to provide some practical advice on each of these three stages of the research process. I began by outlining a three-step action plan to start your assignment. Specifically, you need to clarify what is required of you academically (e.g. with regard to the practical parameters and word length of the assignment, existence of deadlines and whether your supervisor will be assigned or self-selected), choose a feasible topic (e.g. by consulting relevant staff) and to specify your research question(s) as accurately as possible. Remember that you will only make progress in your work when you have identified a clear and precise research question (e.g. 'what caused the Great Famine of the 1840s in Ireland?') as distinct from a more general research topic (e.g. Irish history of the nineteenth century). As I explained, most difficulties experienced by research students may be traced back to this point. In the next section, I presented some practical advice on gathering and evaluating relevant information for your assignment. This data gathering stage involves at least four components: conducting background reading, evaluating this information, taking relevant notes and documenting your reference sources correctly. Having performed these activities, the next step is to write a first draft of your work. As I indicated, the main purpose of this draft is to clarify your thinking *for yourself* – not for the reader. Finally, on the basis that all good writing involves *rewriting*, I explained how to prepare a final version of your work.

10. Exams Kill or Exam Skill? Doing Your Best When It Matters Most

Introduction

Examinations are an integral part of university life. Without them, nepotism would surely reign and it would be '*who* you know' rather than '*what* you know' that would matter academically. But the possession of relevant knowledge does not guarantee exam success. Instead, good results depend significantly on how well you can organise and express your knowledge on the big day. In short, you will receive marks *not* for what you know – but for how well you *transmit* that knowledge under examination conditions. Accordingly, the purpose of the present chapter is to explain how to do your best when it matters most by preparing properly and by developing the habit of sticking to the point when answering questions.

This chapter is organised as follows. In the beginning, I shall consider the purpose of exams and the origins of exam anxiety. Then, I shall suggest some practical techniques for controlling this nervousness. Next, I shall provide some tips on effective revision for exams. After that, I shall present a checklist of things to do before and during exams. Finally, I shall explore the issue of exam 'post-mortems' and offer some advice on what to do if you did not perform as well in your exams as you had hoped.

What is the purpose of exams?

Exams serve many functions in universities. For example, they are used to facilitate selection decisions, to ensure quality control of degree standards and to provide academic feedback to students and staff. But above all, they are designed to assess your *understanding* of what you have learned in a specific course of study. Therefore, exams are best regarded as formal opportunities for you to show what you know – rather than as attempts to find out what you do *not* know. Therefore, they should be seen as challenges rather than threats (see Chapter 6). Unfortunately, this distinction is lost by students who ask such questions as: 'Will I lose marks in an exam if I make a mistake?' This question suggests a false assumption that one starts with full marks in an exam but is then penalised cumulatively for errors! In fact, you start with *zero* marks in an exam but receive *credit* for every piece of relevant information that you provide in answer to the questions asked. In other words, examiners want to *give* marks to you – not to take them away.

In view of the perceived threat which they carry, exams are potentially stressful situations. In fact, coming up to exam time, university counselling services are routinely swamped by people seeking help for such stress-related problems as insomnia, headaches, panic attacks and depression. And they're just the staff! But much of this exam stress is controllable. And by understanding where it comes from, we can learn to make our nervous energy work *for* us rather than against us. So, what is anxiety and why is it generated by exams?

Anxiety

Anxiety is a fear reaction which we experience whenever we interpret a particular person, event or situation as posing a *threat* to us in some way. This threat may be based on realistic or on imaginary fears. For example, if you are a passenger in a speeding car under the control of a drunken driver, then you have a valid reason to be anxious about your safety! But on other occasions, the anxiety which we experience may be completely disproportionate to the realistic danger involved. To illustrate, some people may freeze in terror when they see a harmless spider in the shower. Here, the fear is caused by the *belief* that spiders are unpleasant or dangerous rather than by the actual threat posed by the spider itself. Similarly, exams might frighten us because we believe that our lives will be destroyed if we fail them. Here, the perceived threat comes from thinking too far ahead – worrying about the future rather than tackling the present. Therefore, we can *make ourselves* anxious by the way in which we interpret situations like exams.

Anxiety affects how we feel, think and behave. To begin with, it can produce an unpleasant sensation of bodily tension as well as feelings of agitation and panic. Next, anxiety hampers our thinking and decision-making skills. An anxious student may not perceive an important phrase (e.g. 'compare and contrast') in an exam question because his or her concentration beam has narrowed due to nervousness. Perhaps the best way to counteract this problem is to underline key words to ensure maximum focus. Finally, anxiety can affect the tempo of our behaviour. For example, it may speed up our writing so that it becomes illegible.

So far, you may have concluded that anxiety is an unhelpful emotion – something to be eliminated, if possible. But this idea is wrong. Psychologically, being nervous simply means that you *care* about the results of what you are doing. But such care is misplaced unless you focus only on actions which are under your control. Interestingly, a certain amount of arousal is necessary before any important performance in order to energise our bodies. Therefore, you should never worry about having a pounding heart on the day of an exam. Instead, you should say to yourself, 'Good! My heartbeat shows that my body is fired up and ready for action!'. Without such nervous excitement, you would feel lethargic, flat and unable to rise to the occasion. But why do exams trigger anxiety at all?

What is exam anxiety?

We tend to take exam anxiety for granted. But what causes it? Research suggests that exams tend to make us feel anxious for two reasons. On the one hand, we tend to fear exams, as well as job interviews, because they are formal evaluative situations whose results can be important to our lives. But on the other hand, exam anxiety can arise from discrepancies between the conditions under which we study and those in which we are tested. To explain, you may like to study in a familiar place, with a cup of coffee by your side and your books or notes piled high on your desk – perhaps even soothed by the comforting sound of your favourite background music. But pause for a moment to consider the conditions under which you will be examined: a silent but crowded hall with no background music, no coffee and, worst of all, no notes beside you! Is it any wonder that your mind triggers an alarm response when it notices this stark contrast between your study and exam conditions? Unfortunately, this alarm response seems to be contagious. To illustrate, what do most students do when they receive their exam paper? Curiously, they tend to take a quick glance at the emotional reactions of their classmates to the paper – and if they detect fear, then panic spreads like wild-fire throughout the exam hall, but please don't test this observation for yourself!

To summarise, exams are stressful not only because they evaluate us but also because they require us to perform under conditions which differ significantly from those in which our study occurred. But as these sources of anxiety differ from each other, they should be *treated* differently. To explain, you should be glad of the fact that your body becomes energised at the prospect of doing an exam. But you should try to reduce discrepancy anxiety by studying as often as possible under exam-like conditions (e.g. checking what you can remember about a topic without consulting your summary notes).

How to control your anxiety about exams

Students cope with exam anxiety in many different ways. Some people try to convince themselves that exams are not worth worrying about. After all, they represent only a checkpoint on their journey – not the final destination. Although this attitude is helpful, it does not indicate what to *do* if anxiety strikes. Other students hope that anxiety will go away if it is ignored. Unfortunately, this view is counter-productive because 'bottled up' anxiety will always express itself later. A third way of coping with exam anxiety is to make excuses in advance (e.g. 'My lecturers were useless' or 'I haven't opened a book. I know I'm going to fail'). These excuses are often accompanied by self-defeating actions which sabotage students' own performances. For example, a student might avoid studying for an exam until the last minute so that s/he can attribute the subsequently poor performance to a lack of time to prepare properly. This habit of using excuses before important performance is called self-handicapping and should be eliminated as it prevents people from working on their weaknesses.

What is the best way to deal with exam anxiety? Two steps are required. First, you have to look at exams as challenges rather than as threats. And second, you have to establish control over the exam situation (Moran, 1994).

Exams as opportunities

Look at exams as *opportunities* to show what you know or have learned rather than as tests of what you do *not* know. This change in perception is important because it encourages you to take appropriate actions (e.g. to check that you can recall the contents of your summary sheets without the aid of notes) rather than to worry yourself into inertia.

Establish control over the exam situation

As most anxiety arises from a fear of the unknown, it is vital to establish as much control as possible over the exam situation. This can be done in two ways. First, equip yourself with knowledge about the nature and location of the exam. For example, by visiting the exam hall in advance you can familiarise yourself with its layout and atmosphere. This visit will alleviate some potential discrepancy anxiety (see p. 138). In addition, you must learn to control your own behaviour and to ignore what other people do in the exam. For example, do not look around you in the exam hall when the papers are handed out and do not pay any attention to students who request extra paper from the invigilators. Remember that it is the *quality* rather than quantity of the answer that attracts good marks. In any case, many 'hand raisers' write on only one side of a page or perhaps skip every second line of their answer book. So be selfish in an exam – ignore everyone else.

If neither of these strategies seems to work in alleviating your exam-anxiety, then it may be helpful to discuss your problems with a member of the academic staff and/or with a counsellor in your university. Asking for professional help is an important step in solving any problem.

It's best to revise in silence because you will be tested under silent conditions in the exam hall

Effective revision for exams

In Chapter 5, I explained the PQRR approach to reading. Briefly, this technique emphasises the importance of reviewing (or revising) what you have learned in relation to your study questions. Accordingly, revision is not something that one only does before important exams – it is an extension of the art of reading. The term revision refers to a form of checking. More precisely, it involves reviewing your understanding of what you have learned. It does *not* mean either learning the material for the very first time or else trying to drum it into your mind by passive repetition.

Effective revision involves a sequence of four steps: reviewing the course; checking that you understand relevant course material (e.g. notes from lectures and books); summarising key points in the form of possible exam answers; and testing your ability to reproduce these outline answers under exam-like conditions.

Step 1: Review the scope of the course

In the first stage of your revision, the main objective is to obtain a quick overview of the course so that you can break it into sections, themes or categories. This reorganisation of your course should be guided by the following questions.

What is the scope of the syllabus?

Before you agree to undertake a task, it is wise to establish exactly what it involves. In other words, what topics on the course are examinable? Try to answer this question both by reading through all relevant course outlines and reading lists. You should also consult academic staff members to establish whether or not all the topics on the course are examinable.

What topics and questions have been examined in recent years?

A good way of getting a feel for a course is to skim through typical questions that have been asked on it in recent years. Has the exam rubric (i.e. the arrangement of the questions and any stipulations about the choices to be made) changed from year to year? Is there any pattern evident in the type of questions that are asked from year to year?

What is the best way to organise my notes for each topic?

Classifying information is a useful way of preparing your mind to learn it. Try to classify your notes by theme using separate folders for all relevant lecture notes, course handouts, photocopied articles and other material (e.g. textbook chapters) for each section of the course.

Step 2: Check your understanding of course content

The next stage of revision involves checking your understanding of your material. Looking for common themes in your notes is helpful for two reasons. First, it reduces the amount of detail that you will have to remember and secondly, it makes your revision more abstract. Both of these advantages will serve you well in exams. Having classified your notes, you should check the quality of your understanding by approaching your academic staff with specific questions and/or by forming a study group (a group of classmates who meet regularly to exchange notes and help each other). Although such groups are useful if you do not wish to revise in isolation, they must be complemented by individual study. Remember that in order to achieve the personal goals that you have set for yourself (see Chapter 2), private study can never be replaced by group learning.

Step 3: Make summary answers as possible exam questions

Revision requires the construction of one page summary sheets (see also Chapter 5) for each topic on the course. These summaries provide skeletal answers that can be fleshed out in the exam itself. Ideally, these pages should contain key words which indicate:

- a concise statement of the question underlying this topic/issue/ theory

- key definitions and assumptions

- a list of important features/relevant research findings

- a summary of points of disagreement/controversies

- a brief list of criticisms/evaluative comments

- conclusions

The questions which guide such summary sheets could come from previous years' exam questions or else from the titles of topics on the syllabus.

Step 4: Test yourself under exam-like conditions

Testing your ability to recall your summary sheets is a very helpful revision strategy – especially when it is undertaken under simulated exam conditions. Therefore, make sure to include in every revision session an attempt to recall the main ideas from your summary sheet on a specific topic. This could be done quite easily while travelling on a bus or train or while waiting for a friend in a coffee shop. Remember that the more regularly you review your summary notes,

*You can revise by looking over
your summary sheets at any time!*

the better your memory for them will be in an exam (see the principle of 'distributed learning' in Chapter 3, pp. 34–6).

Testing your skill in recalling summary sheets is beneficial for two reasons. First, it allows you to find out what you really know or can produce when you are forced to reply on your memory rather than on the notes that lie open in front of you. One of the biggest shocks awaiting most students is the discovery, in an exam, that they did not know the material as well as they had previously believed. Second, one of the best ways to counteract pressure situations (such as exams) is to practise under conditions which simulate the main difficulties involved (in this case, the task of marshalling your memories and thoughts under time constraints). This 'adversity training' gives you the confidence to look at exams as nothing more than familiar testing situations. Some practical suggestions for testing yourself when revising are contained in Box 10.1 overleaf.

Box 10.1	How to test yourself during revision

1. *Using a blank sheet of paper, find out how much of your summary sheet you can recall. Note any discrepancies or inaccuracies carefully as these may be the points that you would omit in an exam.*

2. *Try solving a problem or exercise from your textbook and then compare your answer with that in the book.*

3. *Check your ability to define a technical concept without the aid of your notes. Then, compare your version with the definition in the textbook.*

4. *Cover up an important diagram in your textbook and see if you can reproduce it from memory alone.*

Last-minute tips: The night before the exam

What should you do on the night before an exam? Here are some practical tips.

• Make sure that you know the date, time and location of the exam. Check that you know what subject or which part of the course will be examined.

• Glance over previous years' exam papers in this subject in order to get a flavour of the structure of the paper and the type of questions usually asked.

• Work out how many questions you will have to answer and how much time to allocate to each of them.

• Read over your summary sheets for each major topic or theme and test your ability to recall the material in them. Check that you can expand the abbreviations and acronyms that you use. For example, can you remember what the acronym PQRR stands for? (see Chapter 5, pp. 60–4).

• For each topic, make sure that you know what key points you wish to make about the topic and what evidence you can cite in support of them.

- Pack all your essential equipment for the exam (pens, pencils, ruler, calculator, dictionary) into your bag and make sure to include also some form of identification (e.g. student card and exam number). This identification may be required before you enter the exam hall.

- Decide what clothes to wear to the exam on following day. If possible, pick comfortable clothes which are light and layered.

- Resist the temptation to study late into the night on the evening before an exam. Last-minute cramming is not only exhausting – it can also lead to confusion and possible exam blanks on the following day. Going for a relaxing walk is a useful thing to do on the night before an exam.

- Set your alarm early so that you will have plenty of time to get ready for the exam. If you cannot fall asleep, or are tossing and turning all night, try not to worry unduly. This restlessness simply means that you are concerned about your performance – which is a lot better than not caring at all! Your body is a self-correcting system which will restore your sleep balance over the next few nights. *Never* take sleeping pills or unprescribed medication on the night before an exam. These drugs tend to make people feel groggy and lethargic on the following day – hardly the ideal state of mind in which to sit an exam.

On the day of the exam

On the day of the exam, you should follow a definite routine which might include the following steps.

- Wake up early, freshen up with a shower and have a nourishing breakfast.

- Choose the clothes that you had planned to wear. It is advisable to dress in layers of clothes which can be added to or removed conveniently depending on the temperature of the exam hall.

- Skim swiftly through your condensed notes/summary sheets – but do not look at new material in case it might intimidate or confuse you.

- Next, check that you have packed all your exam materials (especially pens, calculator and identification card) into your bag.

- Make your way to the exam hall so that you will arrive about 20 minutes before the exam starts. This period of time is desirable because it is long enough to enable you to become accustomed to the exam atmosphere, but short enough to prevent you from becoming overwhelmed by the anxiety transmitted by any scaremongers in the class.

- During this period, you may wish to have a chat with some of your classmates or else review your summary sheets again. It is not a good idea to review textbooks at this stage because they are too detailed and might cause you to lose your confidence when you see something that you cannot understand or have not prepared properly.

What to do during the exam

Under the stress of exams, people often forget to perform intended actions. Perhaps the best antidote to this problem is to follow a consistent *routine* as much as possible in the exam hall. Adhering to a routine is beneficial because it will focus your mind on the task to be done – not on any doubts or worries which may be at the back of your mind. The key words in this routine are reading, planning, writing and checking.

Before walking into the exam hall, make sure that you are not carrying any exam notes with you. Leave them outside the hall – otherwise you may be accused of cheating. Also, it is a good idea to visit the toilet – three hours is a long time! Next, find your exam desk, sit down and lay out your pens, pencils and identification card in front of you. Look for the clock. If you cannot see it, you should leave your watch down on the desk in a visible location so that you can consult it easily during the exam. Then, take a few deep breaths and say to yourself 'This is an opportunity to show what I've learned. I've prepared well for this moment and I'm going to keep writing until the exam is over'. Wait for any announcements to be made and for the exam papers to be distributed to you. Most essay-type exams have a three-hour time limit and 3–4 questions to be answered. In order to do your best in this situation, you must have a plan for using your time efficiently. Here are some suggestions for what to do after you have received your paper:

- Be glad that you are feeling slightly anxious. Remember that nervous excitement is a sign that your body is 'revved up' and ready to perform.

- Check that you have received the correct exam paper. Sometimes mistakes can occur at this stage – so be attentive.

- Keep your head down and focus only on your own behaviour. Do not allow yourself to be distracted by the sights and sounds around you. Remember that what you do *right now* is all that matters – so use the concentration techniques that I explained in Chapter 6. Ignore the reactions of other students to the paper – it's what *you* do that counts.

- Write your name and details (e.g. exam number) on your script.

- Pay special attention to the rubric (instructions at the top of the paper) specifying the number of questions which you are obliged to answer. Find out whether or not there are any questions on the reverse side of the paper (because in the heat of the moment, anxious students may forget to turn over the paper). Establish which of the questions are optional and which ones are compulsory.

- Spend 3–5 minutes reading the entire paper from beginning to end. You will probably experience a curious mixture of surprise (but hopefully, not shock!) and relief when you see the paper. The surprise may come from the absence of certain topics that you had prepared for and had expected to appear on the paper. But some relief is also likely to occur when you note that certain familiar topics or phrases have been included in the questions. But be careful to note the precise question being asked about these topic. If you are anxious and 'primed' to see a topic that you had prepared, there is a big danger that you will rush into it without taking into account the examiners' angle on the question. To overcome this problem, you should underline each key word in the questions that you select.

- Having decided which questions you feel that you know most about, decide which questions you intend to tackle. It is better to start with the question that you know most about and to leave the most difficult one until last.

- Underline key words (e.g. '*Compare* and *contrast* the *poems* of *Yeats* and *Heaney*') in the title of each of your selected questions in order to make sure that you understand fully what is expected of you and to ensure that you maintain relevance in your answer. If possible, try to allocate a different paragraph to each of the key words in your answer (see also p. 128).

- As I said, start with the question that appears easiest. Also, put a finishing time beside each question to prevent you from spending too long on it.

- Write the number of the question you are answering clearly at the top of the page. But do not waste any time in copying out the text of question.

- Answer the question that you were asked – not the one that you would *like* to have been asked! Even the best students fall prey to the trap of saying to themselves 'I've spent a long time preparing this topic so the examiner is going to get all of my prepared answer to it – no matter what the question is!' Of course, this strategy is counter-productive. It shows that the student has 'answers in search of questions' rather than 'questions in search of answers' (see also p. 63). Your task in an exam is not to summarise the notes that you have lying outside the exam hall – but instead, to use your notes as the scaffolding on which to build your answer. Therefore, you must respond to the wording of the question. The trick here is to weave your prepared answer into the questions asked. In other words, most good answers in an exam are a blend of prepared material (specifically, the skeleton summary sheets that you have used in your revision) and thinking on the spot. The main trap to avoid in this regard is that of neglecting key words in the questions and presenting a pre-packaged but largely irrelevant answer.

- If a question has several different parts, make sure that you cover each one as well as possible.

- To ensure that you stick to the point, jot down any relevant ideas you can think of and make a brief answer plan at the beginning of your answer. Although it is tempting to rush headlong into any question that seems vaguely familiar (especially since other students always seem to be able to write faster than oneself), the time you spend planning your answer is well spent. In particular, it helps in two ways. First, plans serve as a reminder of key points to include in your answer. In addition, it will prevent you from the chief peril of excessive enthusiasm – namely, wandering off the point.

- Try to attack the question from different perspectives, allocating a separate paragraph for each point. This format allows the marker(s) to see each point clearly and facilitates marking.

- Check your progress regularly by making sure that you are sticking to your 'answer plan'.

- A list of typical words and phrases used in exams together with their meaning is provided in Box 10.2.

Box 10.2 — *What do the examiners want? Decoding the meaning of exam questions*

In order to perform well in examinations, you need to make sure to answer the question that you have been asked. But what exactly do examiners mean when they use certain words and phrases? Below is a glossary of 'exam language' (based on Acres, 1984; Deem, 1993; Deese & Deese, 1994; Marshall & Rowland, 1993).

Word/Phrase	**Meaning**
Compare and contrast	*Present both the similarities and the differences between two or more things*
Criticise	*Evaluate a topic or question using relevant evidence and arguments. Give your own view supported by relevant evidence*
Define	*Explain the precise meaning of a given term/phrase*
Describe	*Give a detailed account of*
Discuss	*Tease out different aspects of the topic. Present reasons for and against the topic/argument. Be analytical*
Evaluate/ review	*Examine both sides of an issue or argument. Assess the strengths and weaknesses of the topic. Include your own views substantiated with evidence*
Explain	*Give reasons and/or evidence to support your account of the topic*

Give an account of	*Describe the topic in detail*
Illustrate	*Explain using appropriate examples/diagrams*
Interpret	*Make clear and explicit the meaning of something*
Outline	*Organise your answer to indicate the main features/facts of, or general principles underlying, a given topic*
State	*Present a clear and brief account*
Summarise	*Provide a concise account of the main points*
Trace	*Describe the historical development of*

- If possible, use short sentences when writing. This habit reduces the likelihood of making mistakes (see Box 9.3, p. 126) which confuse both yourself and the examiners.

- Get into the habit of using transition (signpost) words and phrases such as 'for example', 'first . . . second . . . ', 'specifically', 'therefore', 'in summary' as devices to focus your attention and that of the examiner on the most important parts of your answer.

- Try to include a critical evaluation of the material as often as possible. This evaluation may take the form of questioning assumptions/methods, indicating areas of disagreement among relevant researchers or comparing and contrasting rival theories. Remember, however, that such evaluation must always be supported by evidence or arguments. Otherwise, it will be dismissed as a mere opinion.

- If you include any diagrams or graphs, make sure that they are labelled clearly. Failure to indicate what the diagram means suggests a lack of understanding of the material.

- Keep checking that you have not exceeded your proposed finishing time for your answer. If you go beyond the budgeted time, then you should leave a reasonable space and begin the next question. You can always come back to the unfinished one later.

- Try to keep your writing clear and legible.

- If you need more paper, please raise your non-writing hand and wait for the invigilator to come down to your desk.

- Always hand up your 'rough work' in an exam. The notes which it contains may gain additional marks for you.

- If you finish before the exam is over, then review your work to see if there is anything else you can add to your answers.

- Keep writing and stay in the exam hall until you are asked to stop. Sit in your desk until the invigilator collects your paper. Check that your name and exam number are clearly indicated on the answer script.

What to do if you run out of time

As time is a precious commodity in an exam, it must be budgeted carefully. Unfortunately, many students find themselves running out of it as the exam comes to an end. By itself, this pressure of time is not necessarily a bad sign. After all, it could mean that one has a lot of knowledge to impart in the exam. But it could also suggest that one has spent too long on one question to the detriment of others. If this happens, what should you do? The only solution here is to write brief notes which provide an elaboration of your answer plan. If necessary, you could also direct the attention of the examiner to any notes which you may have included in any rough work sheets that you worked on during the exam. It is essential to hand up these sheets as well as any other official exam material.

If you write notes for an answer, try to explain key points as concisely as possible. Under no circumstances should you waste time in writing such phrases as 'I have no time left'! These phrases are not only a waste of valuable time (as they are not relevant to the content of your answer) but are also a source of irritation to examiners.

Before I conclude this section, it is important to address an important question: what are the main reasons why students fail exams? If we can identify these pitfalls then perhaps we can learn to avoid them.

Why do students fail exams? Some pitfalls to avoid

Why do people fail exams? Some of the most common reasons for failure are listed in Box 10.3 overleaf.

Box 10.3 Why do people fail exams? Common pitfalls to avoid

Students fail exams for many reasons. The most common of these difficulties are listed below. Make sure that you do not fall into any of these exam traps.

1. *Inadequate preparation – not having enough knowledge to answer the questions asked*

2. *Not reading the exam question(s) correctly (e.g. rushing into a question without considering its wording/context)*

3. *Failing to answer the required number of questions (e.g. leaving a 'blank' on an exam script or providing an answer that is too short and superficial)*

4. *Irrelevance/failing to answer the question asked (e.g. ignoring certain key words in the exam question, including quotations that are not relevant to the question under discussion, failing to provide sufficient evidence to support arguments)*

5. *Inability to apply what one has learned in the course (e.g. no evidence of understanding basic principles explained in lectures/ reading)*

6. *Excessive repetition (making the same point again and again does not merit extra marks)*

7. *Inefficient use of exam-time (e.g. spending too long on one question causes such problems as losing potential marks on other questions and generating stress from the discovery that you're running out of time)*

8. *Poor presentation of work (e.g. sloppy and disorganised appearance of text, no paragraphs, rambling sentences, presenting abbreviated notes only)*

9. *Not finishing the paper/Leaving before the exam is over (remember – you can only get marks for what you write down!)*

In summary, this section has provided some practical advice on what to do and what *not* to do when sitting exams. But this is not the end of the story as there are two more issues to be considered. These issues, which are concerned with what can happen after your exams are over, involve 'post-mortems' and exam results.

After the exam: Post-mortems

We all know that there is little to be gained by doing post-mortems on exams which have been completed. There are two main reasons for this belief. First, as you cannot change the past, there is little point in torturing yourself by reminding yourself about what you should have included in the answer. Second, and somewhat surprisingly, you may not be a good judge of the quality of what you have written in the exam. Indeed, research suggests that most students are inaccurate in their recall of what they actually wrote in the exam. Therefore, your worries about what you wrote in an exam are rarely justified by the facts. Nevertheless, it is natural for you to want to know what your classmates thought of the exam and how they performed. Accordingly, it is no harm to exchange a few words with them about the test. It is unwise, however, to engage in a detailed question-by-question analysis of the paper as it is only likely to cause you to regret your mistakes or omissions.

Perhaps the best thing to do after an exam is to take some gentle physical exercise which will help you to 'warm down' after the intense experience of answering questions under time pressure. Later, you may wish to focus on the next paper to be tackled in your exams. Remember – concentrate on one exam at a time: don't look too far ahead or you may become downhearted.

Learning from exam results: What if I fail or do badly?

One of the paradoxes of university life is that students often exper-ience a sense of anti-climax rather than relief when they finish their exams. Usually, this feeling stems from a combination of cumulative fatigue and a failure to plan routine activities beyond the exam period. But sooner or later, you will obtain the results of your exams. So, what is the best way to interpret them – especially if you fail or do worse than you had expected?

As I have emphasised repeatedly throughout this book (e.g. see Chapter 6), we are influenced more by the way in which we *inter-pret* events than by the actual events themselves. Therefore, it is vital to regard exam results merely as a source of *feedback* on your *performance* on a particular occasion rather than an some infallible diagnosis of your ability for the rest of your life! On that basis, you should always seek advice or clarification from your academic department as soon as your results become available. In particular, you should:

- Establish as much factual information as possible about your exam performance (e.g. your marks on each section/paper) and the options that are open to you (e.g. do you have to repeat the exam(s) or is compensation possible?).

- Ask the staff for specific advice about how to improve your performance/marks the next time. For example, do they recommend that you should seek tutorial help from a postgraduate student? If so, can they recommend a suitable person for you?

- Find out how soon you can repeat any exam(s) that you have failed. In addition, what steps should you take to register officially for these repeat exams in the university?

Apart from this advice, there is another matter to consider. Sometimes, the disappointment of exam results comes not from being blocked from some career-relevant path or decision, but from social comparison processes. You may feel despondent because you did worse than your friends or classmates. Although this feeling is understandable (especially if they seem to have done less study for the exams than you did), remember that you should focus only on what you can control – not on what happens to someone else. In any case, you must be prepared to take responsibility for your failures as well as your successes. Therefore, try to be self-motivated – not influenced by what happens to other people in exams. In summary, it is up to *you* whether you regard results as a temporary setback or as a final judgement on you as a person (Butler & Hope, 1995).

Summary

Successful performance in exams depends almost as much on strategic factors (e.g. exam skills, such as the capacity to analyse the key words of a question and to 'stick to the point' when answering it) as on the possession of relevant academic knowledge. In short, it is not what you know that counts in an exam – but how well you can express that knowledge on the big day. Remember that marks are awarded only for *evidence* which you provide of your knowledge and understanding. Unfortunately, exams are potentially stressful experiences which can hamper your ability to explain what you know. Therefore, the present chapter offered some practical advice about what to do before and during exams in order to improve your chances of doing well. It also addressed the question of how to interpret exam results as feedback on a specific performance rather than as an infallible diagnosis of your 'true' ability. In the first section, I explained why exams are necessary and considered the main origins of exam anxiety. As I indicated, one reason for this nervousness is that people tend to study under conditions which differ significantly from those encountered in the exam hall. So the more this discrepancy anxiety is reduced by simulating exam conditions in one's studies, the less stress will be triggered by the exam environment. After that, I provided some practical techniques for controlling exam anxiety. These techniques included reinterpreting exams as opportunities rather than as threats and establishing as much control as possible over the exam situation in advance of the big day. In the next section, I presented some tips on effective revision for exams. Here, I covered such steps as reviewing the scope of the course, checking your understanding of what you have learned, making summary notes and testing your ability to recall material under exam-like conditions. Then, based on the idea that a routine approach can counteract stress, I provided a practical checklist of things to do both *before* and *during* exams. In the final section, I explored the issue of exam post-mortems and offered some practical advice on what to do if your exam results were not as good as you had hoped.

References

Acres, D. (1984). *Exams Without Anxiety*. Stoke-on-Trent: Deanhouse.

Annett, J. (1991). Skill acquisition. In J. E. Morrison (Ed.), *Training for Performance: Principles of Appplied Human Learning* (pp. 13–51). Chichester: John Wiley.

Bahrick, H. P., & Phelps, E. (1987). Retention of Spanish vocabulary over eight years. *Journal of Experimental Psychology: Learning, Memory and Cognition*, 13, 344–9.

Barrass, R. (1982). *Students Must Write*. London: Methuen.

Bernstein, D. A., Clarke Stewart, A., Penner, L. A., Roy, E. J., & Wickens, C. D. (2000) *Psychology* (5th ed.). New York: Houghton-Mifflin.

Beyerstein, B. L. (1999). Whence cometh the myth that we only use 10% of our brains? In S. D. Sala (Ed.), *Mind Myths: Exploring Popular Assumptions About the Mind and Brain* (pp. 3–24). Chichester: John Wiley..

Blaxter, L., Hughes, C., & Tight, M. (1996). *How to Research*. Buckingham: Open University Press.

Boland R. (1999). Making magic. *The Irish Times*, Weekend Supplement, 4 December, p. 6.

Borges, J. L. (1970). Funes the memorious. In D. A. Yates & J. E. Irby (Eds), *Labyrinths: Selected Stories and Other Writings*. Harmondsworth, Middlesex: Penguin Books (pp. 87–95).

Bransford, J. D., & Johnson, M. K. (1972). Contextual prerequisites for understanding: Some investigations of comprehension and recall. *Journal of Verbal Learning and Verbal Behaviour*, 11, 717–26.

Bransford, J. D., & Stein, B. S. (1984). *The Ideal Problem Solver: A Guide for Improving Thinking, Learning and Creativity*. New York: W. H. Freeman.

Brown, A. L., & Day, J. D. (1983). Macrorules for summarising texts: The development of expertise. *Journal of Verbal Learning and Verbal Behaviour*, 22, 1–14.

Browne M. N., & Keeley, S. M. (1994). *Asking the Right Questions: A Guide to Critical Thinking* (4th ed.). Englewood Cliffs, N J: Prentice Hall.

Bryson, M., Bereiter, C., Scardamalia, M., & Joram, E. (1991). Going beyond the problem as given: Problem solving in expert and novice writers. In R. J. Sternberg & P. A. Frensch (Eds), *Complex Problem Solving: Principles and Mechanisms*. Hillsdale, N J: Lawrence Erlbaum.

Bull, S. J., Albinson, J. G., & Shambrook, C. J. (1996). *The Mental Game Plan*. Eastbourne, East Sussex: Sport Dynamics.

Burgess, A. (1966). *New York Times Book Review*, 4 December.

Butler, G., & Hope, T. (1995). *Manage Your Mind*. Oxford: Oxford University Press.

Carlson, N. R., & Buskist, W. (1997). *Psychology: The Science of Behaviour* (5th ed). Boston: Allyn & Bacon.

Collins (1996). *Collins Concise Dictionary of Quotations*. Glasgow: HarperCollins.

Connolly, J. (1996). University daze. Education and Living (supplement to *The Irish Times*), 1 October, pp. 2–3.

Cryer, P. (1996). *The Research Student's Guide to Success.* Buckingham: Open University Press.

Deem, J. (1993). *Study Skills in Practice.* Boston: Houghton Mifflin.

Deese, J., & Deese, E. K. (1994). *How to Study and Other Skills for Success in College* (4th ed.). New York: McGraw-Hill.

Dewey, J. (1933). *How We Think: A Restatement of the Relation of Reflective Thinking to the Education Process.* Boston: Heath.

Dooling, D. J., & Lachman, R. (1971). Effects of comprehension on retention of prose. *Journal of Experimental Psychology, 88,* 216–22.

Ebbinghaus, H. (1885/1964). *Memory: A Contribution to Experimental Psychology.* New York: Dover.

Ericsson, A. (1996). *The Road to Excellence.* Hove, East Sussex: Psychology Press.

Foegelin, R. J., & Sinnott-Armstrong, W. (1991). *Understanding Arguments: An Introduction to Informal Logic* (4th ed.). Orlando, Florida: Harcourt Brace Jovanovich.

Gagné, E. D., Yekovich, C. W., & Yekovich, F. R. (1993). *The Cognitive Psychology of School Learning.* New York: HarperCollins.

Gardner, M. (1981). *Science: Good, Bad and Bogus.* New York: Prometheus.

Gilleece, D. (1996). Breathe deep and be happy with second. *The Irish Times,* 27 September, p. 7.

Gilovich, T. (1991). *How We Know What Isn't So: The Fallibility of Human Reason in Everyday Life.* New York: The Free Press.

Goleman, D. (1995). *Emotional Intelligence.* London: Bloomsbury.

Gruneberg, M. (1985). *Linkword French, German, Spanish, Italian, Greek, Portuguese.* London: Corgi Books.

Hamblin, T. J. (1981). Fake. *British Medical Journal, 283,* 1671–1675.

Hartley, J. (1994). The psychology of successful study. *The Psychologist, 7,* 459–60.

Howe, M. J. A. (1999). *Genius Explained.* Cambridge: Cambridge University Press.

Kolodner, J. (1997). Educational implications of analogy: A view from case-based reasoning. *American Psychologist, 52,* 57–66.

Lee, J. (1996). 'Michael Collins' and the teaching of Irish history. *The Sunday Tribune,* 17 September 1996, p. 16.

Logie, R. H. (1999). Working memory. *The Psychologist, 12,* 174–178.

Marshall, L., & Rowland, F. (1993). *A Guide to Learning Independently* (2nd ed.). Buckingham: Open University Press.

Martin, L. (1986). Eskimo words for snow: A case study in the genesis and decay of an anthropological example. *American Psychologist, 88,* 418–23.

Matlin, M. W. (1998). *Cognition* (4th ed.). Fort Worth: Harcourt Brace.

McBurney, D. H. (1996). *How to Think Like a Psychologist: Critical Thinking in Psychology.* Englewood Cliffs, N J: Prentice Hall.

McGuinness, C. (1996). Teaching thinking: Learning to think – thinking to learn. *The Irish Journal of Psychology, 17,* 1–12.

Moran, A. (1994). Coping with pressure: Some lessons from sport psychology. In C. Keane (Ed.), *Nervous Breakdown.* Dublin: Mercier Press/RTÉ (pp. 195–209).

Moran, A. (1996). *Learn to Concentrate* (Audiotape). Aldergrove, Co. Antrim: Tutorial Services (UK) Ltd (Available from leading bookshops).

References **159**

Moran, A. (1996). *The Psychology of Concentration in Sport Performers: A Cognitive Analysis.* Hove, East Sussex: Psychology Press.

Moran, A., Hassett, J., Murphy, D., Nolan, M., & O'Sullivan, C. (1991). *First Year in UCD: A Report to the Registrar by the Committee on Life and Study in University College, Dublin.* Unpublished research report, Registrar's Office, University College Dublin, 30 April.

Morris, T., & Summers, J. (1995). *Sport Psychology: Theory, Applications and Issues.* Brisbane: John Wiley.

Neimark, E. (1987). *Adventures in Thinking.* New York: Harcourt Brace Jovanovich.

Norman, D. A. (1982). *Learning and Memory.* San Francisco: W. H. Freeman.

Northedge, A. (1990). *The Good Study Guide.* Milton Keynes: Open University Press.

Otway, G. (1999). Clarke enjoys special K day. *The Sunday Times*, 1 August, p. 13.

Palmer, R., & Pope, C. (1984). *Brain Train: Studying for Success.* London: E. & F. N. Spon.

Peoples, D. A. (1988). *Presentations Plus.* New York: John Wiley.

Piaget, J. (1962). *Play, Dreams and Imitation in Childhood.* New York: Norton.

Pinker, S. (1994). *The Language Instinct.* New York: Allen Lane/The Penguin Press.

Pressley, M., & Mc Cormick, C. B. (1995). *Cognition, Teaching and Assessment.* New York: HarperCollins.

Pullum, G. K. (1991). *The Great Eskimo Vocabulary Hoax and Other Irreverent Essays on the Study of Language.* Chicago: University of Chicago Press.

Race, P. (2000). *How to Win as a Final-Year Student: Essays, Exams and Employment.* Buckingham: Open University Press.

Randi, J. (1975). *The Magic of Uri Geller.* New York: Ballantine Books.

Raugh, M. R., & Atkinson, R. C. (1975). A mnemonic method for learning a second language vocabulary. *Journal of Educational Psychology, 67*, 1–16.

Robinson, F. P. (1961). *Effective Study.* New York: Harper & Row.

Roediger, H. L., Capaldi, E. G., Paris, S. G., Polivy, J., Herman, C. P. (1995). *Psychology*, 4th ed. St Paul, Minnesota: West.

Sagan, C. (1987). The fine art of baloney. *Parade*, 1 February, 12–13.

Scott, S. (1999). Out of the Woods. *SportsWrite Magazine*, July, pp. 44–8.

Searlman, A., & Herrmann, D. (1994). *Memory from a Broader Perspective.* New York: McGraw Hill.

Seligman, M. E. P. (1991). *Learned Optimism.* New York: Norton.

Shalvey, J. (1995). Order of the boot. *The Irish Times*, 17 May, pp. 24–5.

Shermer, M. (1997) *Why People Believe Weird Things: Pseudoscience, Superstition and Other Confusions of Our Time.* New York: W. H. Freeman.

Skrabanek, P., & McCormick, J. (1989). *Follies and Fallacies in Medicine.* Glasgow: Tarragon Press.

Sloboda, J. (1986). Reading: A case study of cognitive skills. In A. Gellatly (Ed.), *The Skilful Mind: An Introduction to Cognitive Psychology.* Milton Keynes: Open University Press (pp. 39–49).

Sternberg, R. J. (1988). *The Psychologist's Companion: A Guide to Scientific Writing for Students and Researchers.* Cambridge: Cambridge University Press.

Sternberg, R. J. (1999). *Cognitive Psychology* (2nd ed.). Fort Worth: Harcourt Brace.

Strunk, W., & White, E. B. (1979). *The Elements of Style* (3rd ed.). New York: Macmillan.

Wade, C., & Tavris, C. (1987). *Psychology.* New York: Harper & Row.

Walsh, D., & Paul, R. (1986). *The Goal of Critical Thinking: From Educational Ideal to Educational Reality.* Washington, D.C.: American Federation of Teachers.

Whimbey, A. (1976). *Intelligence Can Be Taught.* New York: Bantam.

Wilding, J., & Hayes, S. (1992). Relations between approaches to studying and note-taking behaviour in lectures. *Applied Cognitive Psychology, 6,* 233–46.

Wyatt, D., Pressley, M., El-Dinary, P. B., Stein, S., Evans, P., & Brown, R. (1993). Comprehension strategies, worth, and credibility monitoring, and evaluations: Cold and hot cognition when experts read professional articles that are important to them. *Learning and Individual Differences, 5,* 49–72.

Zechmeister, E. B., & Johnson, J. E. (1992). *Critical Thinking: A Functional Approach.* Belmont, California: Brooks/Cole.

Zimbardo. P. G., Weber, A. L., & Johnson, R. L. (2000). *Psychology* (3rd ed.). Boston: Allyn and Bacon.

Index